# LAKE HOLLYWOOD

BY **JOHN GUARE**

★

★

DRAMATISTS
PLAY SERVICE
INC.

LAKE HOLLYWOOD
Copyright © 2000, John Guare

All Rights Reserved

LAKE HOLLYWOOD was originally produced at the Signature Theater (James Houghton, Founding Artistic Director) in New York City on April 29, 1999. It was codirected by Doug Hughes and Itamar Kubovy; the set design was by David Cosier; the lighting design was by Joe Saint; the costume design was by Teresa Snider-Stein; and the stage manager was Amanda Sloan. The cast was as follows:

## ACT ONE

| | |
|---|---|
| AGNES | Kate Burton |
| ANDREW | Adam Grupper |
| FLO | Amy Wright |
| MRS. LARRY | Pamela Nyberg |
| RANDOLPH | Josh Harto |
| UNCLE AMBROSE | Alan North |

## ACT TWO

| | |
|---|---|
| AGNES | Betty Miller |
| ANDREW | Ralph Waite, then Mason Adams |
| MRS. GARCIA | Pamela Nyberg |
| MR. EDE | Doc Dougherty |
| MRS. HASSELBACH | Amy Wright |
| VINNIE | Doc Dougherty |
| HILDEGARDE | Kate Burton |
| GEORGE | Adam Grupper |
| MONICA | Natalie Paulding |
| WALLY PANTONI | Josh Harto |

LAKE HOLLYWOOD was substantially revised for the Guthrie Theater (Joe Dowling, Artistic Director; David Hawkanson, Managing Director) in Minneapolis, Minnesota, where it opened on February 9, 2000. It was directed by Itamar Kubovy; the set design was by Neil Patel; the lighting design was by Jeff Bartlett; the sound design was by Scott W. Edwards; the costume design was by Rich Hamson; the dramaturg was Michael Lupu; and the stage manager was Martha Kulig. The cast was as follows:

THE YOUNG GIRL/MONICA ................... Britta Lee Nordahl
AGNES ................................................ Sally Wingert
ANDREW ............................................ David Manis
THE MAN/VINNIE ..................................... Terry Hempleman
FLO/MRS. GARCIA ....................................... Marcelline Hugot
MRS. LARRY/MRS. HASSELBACH ........... Elizabeth Norment
RANDOLPH/WALLY PANTONI ........................... Alex Knold
UNCLE AMBROSE/MR. EDE ............................... Clyde Lund
WITNESS #1/HILDEGARDE ...................... Marquetta Senters
WITNESS #2/GEORGE ............................................ Bob Davis

# CHARACTERS

AGNES
ANDREW
THE YOUNG GIRL
MONICA
THE MAN
VINNIE
FLO
MRS. GARCIA
MRS. LARRY
MRS. HASSELBACH
RANDOLPH
WALLY PANTONI
UNCLE AMBROSE
MR. EDE
WITNESS #1
HILDEGARDE
WITNESS #2
GEORGE


All roles double except AGNES and ANDREW:

THE YOUNG GIRL/MONICA
THE MAN/VINNIE
FLO/MRS. GARCIA
MRS. LARRY/MRS. HASSELBACH
RANDOLPH/WALLY PANTONI
UNCLE AMBROSE/MR. EDE
WITNESS #1/HILDEGARDE
WITNESS #2/GEORGE

# LAKE HOLLYWOOD

## Prologue

*The first sound: a sustained single chord. Shimmering. Expectant. Transcendent. Is it the wind through trees? A Young Girl appears. She's fourteen. She wears a bathing suit, circa 1918.*

THE YOUNG GIRL. *(To us:)* Water comes next to air as a life necessity; it should be the best the earth affords. New Hampshire, the Granite State, has water power in abundance. Lake Winnipesaukee which in Indian means The Smile of the Great Spirit is eighty-five square miles of water. It offers natural beauty the like of which is unequaled anywhere in the world. The scent of pines. The glory of the clouds. The purity of the air. Come enjoy the exhilaration of bathing in the healing and invigorating water of a lake such as Winnipesaukee and become one with the smile of the Great Spirit. *(She smiles. Darkness.)*

## ACT ONE

### Scene 1

*A country road. New Hampshire. August. 1940.*

*A car speeds by. Agnes and Andrew, both late thirties, watch it go past. They've just got off a bus. A very hot summer day. Locusts. They're both dressed for the city. She carries the only suitcase and a mesh shopping bag containing groceries. Silence. He is very cross. She's anxiously looking down the road. She sings in a small voice:*

AGNES. "Come on and hear, oh let me take you by the hand."
ANDREW. I must be nuts.
AGNES. They know what time we got off the bus. They'll be here. "Come on and hear, It's the best band in the land."
ANDREW. It's hotter up here than all of New York.
AGNES. Wait till you're in that lake.
ANDREW. We could be at the beach — *(She looks down the road.)*
AGNES. "They can play a bugle call like you never heard before, So natural that you want to go to war." — *(A sudden gust of wind blows by.)*
ANDREW. Wait. Smoke. That's smoke. Smell the smoke?
AGNES. *(Bright.)* Don't smell. It's probably the campgrounds. The Jehovah Witness camp grounds catches on fire at least once a year.
ANDREW. Once a year? The day I come?
AGNES. We live on the lake so if it turns into a forest fire, you jump right in the water. Up there is a pretty little town called The Weirs, and back there is a sweet little town called Alton Bay, and way across the lake is Wolfeboro.
ANDREW. I don't like water where you see the other side. You're a lake person. I'm an ocean person. I love Long Beach, Long Island! When I swim, Europe is over there. Spain! Morocco! Not some Wolfeboro or paltry Alton Bay. Swimming in lakes, you're always seeing the other side, coming out covered with slime from the bottom, oil from the motorboats. Minnows.
AGNES. Okay okay —
ANDREW. No tides. Water always the same height. Full of rowboats. But the ocean! High tide, low tide, filled with sharks and whales and ocean liners. The Île-de-France. Riding the waves —
AGNES. I like watching you ride the waves.

ANDREW. What can you ride in a lake? You're never trapped in the ocean. You know what I think a lake is like?

AGNES. What do you think a lake is like?

ANDREW. Marriage is like a lake.

AGNES. *(Hopeful.)* Oh?

ANDREW. Marriage is always seeing the other side. Marriage is no tides. Marriage is water always the same height. Marriage is minnows. Marriage is rowboats. Marriage is Wolfeboro.

AGNES. Who's talking about marriage?

ANDREW. Nobody. I'm talking about lake people and ocean people. The big difference between —

AGNES. Okay. But you have to go in the water.

ANDREW. You said come up to New Hampshire for a quiet weekend. Do what you want. What I want is not go in a lake. You said they'd pick us up.

AGNES. And I'll keep saying it.

ANDREW. You also keep saying you'll change, you'll change.

AGNES. Ethel Kelly came back from her honeymoon and said all that bedroom stuff was overrated. She came back from Bermuda and said, "Agnes, an overrated sport."

ANDREW. Ethel Kelly is an expert on anything.

AGNES. I'm just quoting Ethel Kelly.

ANDREW. Quote to yourself what you say about cooking. "Try it before you judge it."

AGNES. I'm warming up. Give me time. It's only been three years.

ANDREW. Three years! Jesus, and another stinking day.

AGNES. Today is not just a *day*. Today is August fifteenth. It's my present to you.

ANDREW. Your birthday? Why didn't you tell me?

AGNES. If you was Catholic, you'd know today was the most important day. The Feast of the Assumption. The Blessed Mother of Jesus himself died —

ANDREW. Mary —

AGNES. Mary was dying all alone, and up in heaven Jesus looked down and missed her so much that He, the Son of God, assumed her body up into heaven, like rainwater in reverse, making her the only human being ever to fly to heaven in her very own body. He

9

put her on a golden throne right beside Him and she lives there forever.

ANDREW. She lives up there?

AGNES. Mary was so happy being in heaven with her family that on that day she flew up — today — as a present to the world, she put a miraculous cure in every drop of water all over the world. *(That transcendent chord holds just for a moment.)* The water in every lake, every ocean, every stream, every ripple is holy. You got to go swimming. At least a dunk.

ANDREW. Are you a religious nut?

AGNES. This is true.

ANDREW. How do they know this is true?

AGNES. Because all the apostles were there plus a lot of other people from around who stopped by and they all saw the Blessed Virgin Mary die and then go up in the sky and they looked down in her deathbed and they saw roses. There's pictures of this. Well, paintings. Lovely paintings.

ANDREW. We don't have the Blessed Mother. We were Dutch Reform.

AGNES. But you're not Dutch. Are you?

ANDREW. Where I was raised was Dutch Reform.

AGNES. Where? I still don't know where you were raised.

ANDREW. What is this? "Information Please"?

AGNES. I'd like to know something about you.

ANDREW. Nothing to know. The end. *(The wind blows ominously.)* These mountains. I get to the country, I feel trapped. *(Andrew pulls a flask out of his pocket.)*

AGNES. I beg you — whatever. Whatever whatever *whatever* you do, don't drink.

ANDREW. I'm not drinking. *(He takes a swig.)*

AGNES. Don't give a drink to Uncle Ambrose.

ANDREW. Who?

AGNES. My Uncle Ambrose is allergic. Don't even show him the label of a drink.

ANDREW. It's too hot. *(He puts the flask away.)*

AGNES. "Come on along, come on along." Look! There's huckleberries! They make a great pie.

ANDREW. Deers pee on them.

AGNES. Deers don't pee on huckleberries.

ANDREW. Where's the rest stop?

AGNES. Go over there.

ANDREW. Get poison ivy? *(Andrew goes off, annoyed. Agnes looks around.)*

AGNES. "Come on and hear, come on and hear. Let me take you by the hand." *(A low rumbling sound. Is it distant thunder? A Man appears, dressed in a white linen suit in the style of 1918. Agnes looks up.)*

THE MAN. "Come on and hear, come on and hear." Get in. Get in my car. It has red leather seats. A pretty girl like you shouldn't be walking. You want a ride? Come closer. Smell the leather. "It's the best band in the land." *(Agnes walks towards him, slowly. Andrew returns.)*

ANDREW. Poison ivy all over my private parts. *(The Man is gone. Agnes, wheezing, runs to Andrew and clutches him.)*

AGNES. I want to get home.

ANDREW. New York?

AGNES. No. Here! I hate this part of the road. Let him see you. Let him see I'm protected. Stand close. Don't go away.

ANDREW. You're wheezing — are you all right? *(Agnes pulls away and smiles brightly.)*

AGNES. I'm fine. It's the dust. The heat. I need to get in the water. We can walk by the lake. A good walk. Healthy!

ANDREW. That lake looks like where FDR got polio.

AGNES. Let's start. We'll meet them coming. *(Agnes starts to walk. Andrew stays back.)*

ANDREW. What did you tell them about me?

AGNES. All I could fit on a postcard. A friend would be accompanying me. Meet us.

ANDREW. What kind of friend?

AGNES. I said the truth. An executive with the Monitor and Merrimac Soap Company.

ANDREW. Exec — ! I'm a pen pusher *in* the executive offices!

AGNES. Don't worry. My family don't even know what an executive is. These are country people —

ANDREW. I hope they don't think I'm going to marry you.

AGNES. Nobody thinks anything.

ANDREW. We're just neighbors. You rent a room on the eighth floor. I rent a room on an entirely different floor. The fourth floor.
AGNES. Andrew, it's just a weekend in the country.
ANDREW. Yeah — with a cure in the water. There is a car?
AGNES. And a horse named Beau. And a wagon. And a boat. Lots of ways to escape. Don't worry.
ANDREW. How far is it?
AGNES. Three miles.
ANDREW. Three miles? Twenty city blocks to a mile? That's walking from Fourteenth Street to Seventy-Fourth Street! I'd take a subway! (*They're gone.*)

# Scene 2

*A jaunty Dixieland recording of "The World is Waiting for the Sunrise" coming out of the horn of an old windup Victrola. The ancient machine sits in a rowboat that has been filled with boxes. A rickety house is off to the right. We can see the front door of it. Tall, charred trees stand to the left. A deck, center, is on the lake in the background. A working water pump over there by the trees. Boxes are stacked not only in the rowboat but all over the property as if for a quick move. An enormous piece of furniture, a credenza, is tipped on its side with flotation devices, rubber tires, tarps, tied to it.*

*Flo, Randolph and Mrs. Larry sit on a blanket on the deck. Flo, forties, in a housedress and apron, wears her marcelled grey hair in a severe bun. Mrs. Larry, forties, platinum blonde, elaborate hairdo, wears a leopard-skin coat over her halter and shorts. High heels. She smokes. Randolph is nineteen years old. His head is bandaged like a turban. A bandage is pasted over each eyebrow.*

*At the moment, they are playing charades. Randolph makes sleeping gestures. Flo is deep in the game. Mrs. Larry is bored.*

FLO. Sleep.

RANDOLPH. No!

FLO. You can't call out! *(Randolph puts his bandaged hands alongside his head.)*

FLO. Bandaged hands!

RANDOLPH. No!

MRS. LARRY. Are we playing cards? *(Mrs. Larry has a deep German accent.)*

FLO. This is my house, Mrs. Larry. We are playing charades. I call the shots. Get me? Charades. *(Randolph picks up a baseball bat and swings.)* Baseball!

RANDOLPH. No!

FLO. Golf!

RANDOLPH. No! *(Randolph runs to the lake and splashes water.)*

FLO. Lake!

RANDOLPH. No! *(Randolph folds his hands alongside his head.)*

FLO. I don't know. Headache?

MRS. LARRY. Nap. *(Randolph shakes his head YES! then touches his forearm, his head, his leg.)*

FLO. Leg?

MRS. LARRY. Bone.

RANDOLPH. Yes! *(Randolph swings his bat again.)*

FLO. Hit?

MRS. LARRY. Bat.

RANDOLPH. Yes! *(Randolph splashes water.)*

MRS. LARRY. Water. Napoleon Bonaparte. The Battle of Waterloo! *(Randolph kisses Mrs. Larry deeply. She leans back, very pleased.)*

MRS. LARRY. I'll say this for you, Randy. You know how to kiss. What a banker you'll be.

FLO. He's going to teach in the schools.

MRS. LARRY. Money. Finance. Banking. That's what Randy will do.

FLO. Teach.

MRS. LARRY. He's not teaching. He's too smart for school.

RANDOLPH. I'm with you there!

MRS. LARRY. Without money, you're trapped. I want Randolph to be free. I don't want him to be like me.

FLO. Living on other people's charity? Say it. Say it.

MRS. LARRY. I want to be the one giving out charity. And you know how much I'll give out? None. Either side of charity makes you a Ninety-eight-pound weakling.

FLO. Then I suggest you move out as fast as you can.

MRS. LARRY. To go where? This frying pan. This fire.

RANDOLPH. *(To Mrs. Larry:)* As long as I'm here, this frying pan is your home.

FLO. You can't offer her anything. It's not your home.

RANDOLPH. Not my home! Should I go? Is that what you're telling me? Not my home! Not my home! *(Randolph picks up a suitcase and starts to go.)*

FLO. *(Panic.)* No! Don't even hint that! Don't even —

MRS. LARRY. Make money, Randolph. Money is the only freedom. *(Randolph kisses Mrs. Larry. A deep kiss.)*

FLO. He's opening the hardware store in Wolfeboro, then he's going into politics. *(Randolph kisses Flo. A deep kiss. Mrs. Larry deals.)*

MRS. LARRY. My bones say banker.

FLO. My bones know a *helluva* lot more than your bones —

RANDOLPH. Ladies! I am not going into banking. I am going directly into politics. Politics for me! I want power.

FLO. That's my boy!

MRS. LARRY. You win this round.

FLO. And I own this house. *(Flo holds her cards in one hand and Randolph's cards in her other.)*

MRS. LARRY. Not for long.

FLO. What are you saying?

MRS. LARRY. One diamond.

FLO. What does that mean? Not for long, Randolph? What does that mean?

RANDOLPH. You know I'd feel happier if the house was in my name.

FLO. But Agnes and I own the house together.

RANDOLPH. I don't like that.

FLO. She's my sister. Our parents left us this house.

RANDOLPH. Don't you want me to be happy? Maybe I should go.

FLO. Don't go! I want you to be happy but —

MRS. LARRY. Wait — *(A sharp noise. They freeze in alarm.)*

FLO. I heard a branch crack.

MRS. LARRY. There's somebody out there.

RANDOLPH. Is it the firemen? I want to go back to the fire!

FLO. No! You're not going back to any fire! Hide him! They're not taking you — *(Flo holds Randolph down. Mrs. Larry throws a blanket over a struggling Randolph.)*

RANDOLPH. I want to go back to the fire! *(Agnes and Andrew, dusty, breathless from their hike, come out of the house.)*

AGNES. We're home! *(Flo screams, then bursts out laughing.)*

FLO. You scared the bejesus out — !

AGNES. Everything's out of the house. Oh, it's out here. *(Flo lifts up the blanket, revealing Randolph.)*

RANDOLPH. It's Agnes.

MRS. LARRY. So that's Agnes. Get her to sign the paper.

RANDOLPH. Don't worry!

AGNES. I thought you'd pick us up. We waited and waited at Lawson's Corner.

FLO. Don't have a car! Marty Quinn and the volunteer firemen commandeered the car! Is that a man?

AGNES. This is Andrew!

ANDREW. Hi.

FLO. You walked three miles from Lawson's Corners with a man? Marty Quinn's dragging off every available pair of pants to fight the fire. *(Andrew backs away.)*

RANDOLPH. Welcome to Lake Squamsquam! You want to go back and dig fire trenches?

ANDREW. I don't want to fight any —

AGNES. *(Waves her shopping bag.)* I brought lunch!

FLO. Randolph, you are not going back anywhere near those campgrounds, and we don't need lunch. Randolph rescued two dozen pies from the fire even with his hands burned.

RANDOLPH. Say what you want about those Jehovahs, they bake a good blueberry pie. *(Randolph holds up the stack of pies with his wrists.)*

MRS. LARRY. The rhubarb is a little charred on the sides.

FLO. The rhubarb isn't that charred. Randolph paid his dues. His heroism. This will be very good when he runs for office.

RANDOLPH. I'm going to run for office as soon as I can vote.

AGNES. Randolph? You look so different.

FLO. Randolph had his perfect eyebrows burned off.

RANDOLPH. *(Thrilled.)* Plus I singed my hands!

FLO. He can't even hold cards. I have to hold his cards after the most harrowing night of my life. When the firemen brought him home unconscious, gasping for breath, his face was as black as Al Jolson in *The Jazz Singer.* Black as the ace of spades.

RANDOLPH. Is that a bid?

FLO. No! I'm describing you, lover. Two hearts. No, one heart. *(To Randolph:)* You're bidding one spade.

RANDOLPH. One spade.

MRS. LARRY. Pass.

FLO. Pass. *(Andrew looks around.)*

AGNES. Don't worry, Andrew. The fire usually doesn't come out this far.

FLO. It did this morning! Didn't it stop right there at the trees!

ANDREW. Right there? They're burned.

AGNES. Better to be safe than sorry. Come inside and change.

RANDOLPH. Don't go in the house! You might get trapped in the flames!

FLO. We're ready to evacuate in a moment.

RANDOLPH. If the wind hadn't turned at the very last instant, I would've been cremated. I leaped like a leapfrog out of the way! You might not be so fast!

ANDREW. You may be right — Agnes!

AGNES. Where's Uncle Ambrose? Is he fighting the fire?

FLO. The firefighters have enough trouble without Uncle Ambrose.

AGNES. Ambrose! Uncle Ambrose! *(Her voice echoes over the lake: "Ambrose! Uncle Ambrose!")*

ANDREW. Did I ever tell you how I got trapped in the Parachute Jump, swinging over Coney Island? I'm getting that feeling.

AGNES. Trapped! We're not trapped. *(The wind roars. The sky turns red. Everyone runs in panic.)*

FLO. *(Terrified.)* Oh God!

ANDREW. Is that smoke?

RANDOLPH. Wait. No. Yes.

FLO. Oh God. Oh God. *(The sky returns to normal. The wind settles.)*

RANDOLPH. Quiet. Safe for now. *(They relax. Except for Andrew.)*

AGNES. Let's get in that water!

ANDREW. Could you maybe phone somebody in town and get a report on how the fire's doing?

AGNES. We don't have —

ANDREW. No phone.

FLO. Wouldn't Nellie Cluff love us to get a phone so she can listen in on our entire lives?

AGNES. How is Nellie Cluff? *(To Andrew:)* She runs the general store in Alton.

FLO. Arthritis. Bent over like a pretzel.

AGNES. I'd like to spin over to Alton and see her. We could organize a hayride!

FLO. Wagon's out there. Wheel's off. No hay. Beau died.

AGNES. Beau? You didn't tell me Beau died. Oh Andrew, Beau was the nicest horse ... We do have the boat. We can rent skis over at Alton Bay and go waterskiing.

FLO. Outboard stolen last Labor Day.

RANDOLPH. I blame the Jehovahs. If I'm elected, I'm going to start looking into their finances. Tithing? Ten percent? Something's very fishy.

FLO. Randolph. First things first. Let's get through this day alive. Wait — the wind is shifting — *(The wind roars. The sky turns red. Randolph leaps up, waving his arms.)*

RANDOLPH. Stay back, wind! The wind does what I tell it to! Wind! Back! Back! Change direction! *(The wind settles. The sky returns to normal.)* It obeys me! Relax.

ANDREW. Relax?

FLO. Thank God for you. My miracle!

RANDOLPH. I turned the wind back! I have that power. Don't ask me why. I just have it!

FLO. However, in spite of his magic powers, the fickle wind can change in a second and cremate us into ash! *(Agnes spots the credenza covered with inner tubes and blankets.)*

AGNES. My mother's credenza!

17

ANDREW. Her what?

AGNES. See! A credenza's got shelves on the top half behind glass doors. Open up the bottom part and it's a desk. With a secret drawer to put stuff in. It's mahogany.

FLO. It's *almost* mahogany.

RANDOLPH. We can sail to Europe in it.

AGNES. Mother loved it so.

FLO. It's mine. *(Agnes takes a deep breath and decides to smile.)*

AGNES. We've walked it seems a hundred miles uphill! *(To Andrew:)* Do you want a drink?

ANDREW. You're a mind reader! Yes! I'd love a drink.

AGNES. Where are the glasses?

FLO. In those boxes. We packed away all the china, the family valuables, to fling in the lake.

ANDREW. Where do you go if the flames — ?

FLO. We sit out on the lake in our boat with all our valuables gathered around us, praying flaming pine trees don't topple over on us and crush us. *(Andrew smiles, ashen. Agnes takes out a glass and regards it lovingly.)*

RANDOLPH. Those are *my* glasses.

FLO. Agnes, stop coveting those glasses. The glasses stay here. The credenza stays here. I'd love to get down to New York and see what's she stolen out of here.

AGNES. I'm just admiring them. See, Andrew?

ANDREW. Nice.

AGNES. Beautiful Czechoslovakian glass. Although we're not Czechoslovakian. Poland. Czechoslovakia. I hate to hear the news. Do you ever think sometimes the whole world is on fire?

RANDOLPH. I say two sides to every story. Poland and Czechoslovakia must have asked for it.

AGNES. Hitler is a terrible man.

RANDOLPH. Time will tell. Time will tell.

AGNES. Adolf Hitler wants the world for his own!

FLO. If you're going to bring your New York New Deal doom and gloom up here, find another vacation spot to freeload at. This is a Wendell Willkie house. *(Agnes pumps water and fills the glass.)*

ANDREW. I stay out of politics.

AGNES. Freeload? This is my home. Andrew, this water is like champagne!

FLO. Can't hear you. Concentrating.

MRS. LARRY. *(To Randolph:)* She said "my home." *(Randolph leans on Mrs. Larry.)*

RANDOLPH. Agnes owns half the house.

MRS. LARRY. Half a house doesn't make it her house. Get her to sign the paper.

FLO. There is no muttering in my house. Randolph, Mrs. Larry is not a tree. *(Randolph sits up.)*

AGNES. So you're Mrs. Larry! We missed you at the wedding. *(Mrs. Larry crushes out her cigarette.)*

MRS. LARRY. I spent the wedding day out on Lake Squamsquam, drifting. It was a day of great emotion for me.

FLO. For all of us, Mrs. Larry, for all of us.

MRS. LARRY. We win. We lose.

FLO. Shut up, Mrs. Larry. Four diamonds. No, change that. Five diamonds. *(To Randolph:)* Pass.

RANDOLPH. Pass.

MRS. LARRY. Diamonds is it? This means war. *(Flo, Mrs. Larry and Randolph concentrate on their cards.)*

AGNES. Everybody, I know you're playing the Contract Bridge Olympics but I want you to know Andrew.

FLO. Andrew?

AGNES. You know Velvet Soap? Andrew *is* Velvet Soap. He works in the executive offices of the Monitor and Merrimac Soap —

FLO. We got your postcard.

MRS. LARRY. The executive offices? Well, hello, stranger.

ANDREW. Hello.

MRS. LARRY. A Titan of Finance?

ANDREW. No no —

MRS. LARRY. Or is it a Captain of Industry?

ANDREW. I'm not actually an executive. I work *in* the exec —

MRS. LARRY. The titan is modest.

ANDREW. Maybe I am.

AGNES. Andrew, look at the lake! I prayed the weather would be like this!

FLO. You should have prayed some deranged Jehovah didn't light a match.

MRS. LARRY. All these prayers. I prayed. I didn't pray. Who cares. Let God pray to me. God starts these forest fires to get my attention. You know what I say to God? "God, you don't amuse me." I like to be amused. I'll tell you what amuses me. Money amuses me. Do you like money, Mr. Soap Suds? Come talk to me about money.

ANDREW. You're from someplace —

MRS. LARRY. Berlin.

AGNES. You never told me that.

FLO. That's true. She's from Berlin.

ANDREW. *(Impressed.)* Berlin?

MRS. LARRY. *Unter den Linden.* Strolling with a lover. Living free. Loving free. Who you want. When you want. *(Mrs. Larry takes off her leopard-skin coat and lets it sink to the ground. She stands there in her halter and shorts.)*

FLO. Oh brother.

ANDREW. What memories you must have.

MRS. LARRY. No, no, no. The past is a rich meal. I choke on the past. I don't dine at that table. I live for now.

ANDREW. That's very beautiful. *(Agnes opens her suitcase.)*

AGNES. Andrew, let's get in the water.

FLO. One suitcase?

AGNES. Andrew doesn't own one.

FLO. Doesn't own a suitcase?

ANDREW. I'm an ocean person! Swimming trunks. Stick 'em in my pocket.

FLO. Sharing a suitcase? What have you turned into? You're not living together?

AGNES. Flo! Please! No! We're friends!

ANDREW. Neighbors!

AGNES. Who'd want to live with anyone? I love my independence. I am proud to be a bachelor girl.

FLO. Whatever you say, Miss Off-Center of the Universe.

AGNES. Andrew, come get your trunks. *(Agnes sees Flo and Mrs. Larry staring at Andrew.)*

FLO. Typical Agnes exaggeration. She told me she was bringing up the handsomest man she ever saw, that her heart stood still, that she used to follow him before they met — *(Flo deals. Agnes is stunned.)*

ANDREW. *(To Agnes:)* You did?

MRS. LARRY. Agnes may be right. The way the light falls across your cheekbones. But even Mr. Cheekbones looks like he needs a pick-me-up. *(Mrs. Larry shows a bottle in her purse.)*

ANDREW. Mr. Cheek…? Oh, a pick-me-up!

AGNES. He's my guest, Mrs. Larry.

FLO. Don't be selfish, Agnes. *(Andrew takes a swig from Mrs. Larry's bottle.)*

AGNES. When we get out of the water, we'll have lunch. I brought up the makings of a Waldorf salad which is apples and iceberg lettuce and is all the rage in New York City. We could eat iceberg night and day!

RANDOLPH. Lettuce made of icebergs? *(Agnes pumps water. She cools her face and neck.)*

MRS. LARRY *(To Andrew:)* Do you play charades?

ANDREW. I never learned.

MRS. LARRY. Do you play Monopoly?

ANDREW. It takes too long.

MRS. LARRY. Honeymoon Monopoly. For two. It's fast. I'm a good teacher.

ANDREW. I'm game!

AGNES. Andrew? Could you spare yourself?

ANDREW. *(To Mrs. Larry:)* Yes yes — excuse me one moment — *(Andrew runs to Agnes at the pump. They whisper:)*

AGNES. Andrew, could we please get in the water?

ANDREW. Who is who? Give me a scorecard.

AGNES. Florence is my sister and Randolph is her husband.

ANDREW. Her husband? He's a boy.

AGNES. He's nineteen.

ANDREW. Nineteen?

AGNES. That's not so young.

ANDREW. How old is your sister?

AGNES. She's around maybe — she's forty-one.

ANDREW. Forty-one and nineteen? You don't think that's strange?

AGNES. The water pump got broken. Randolph was the

plumber from the repair shop in Durham. They got talking about bridge. They got married last Valentine's Day. I came up for it. Snow.

ANDREW. And who is Mrs. Larry?

AGNES. Mrs. Larry is Randolph's mother.

ANDREW. Randolph's *mother!* But she looks —

AGNES. She looks about a hundred. That blonde hair.

ANDREW. And she lives with them?

AGNES. *(Whispering ends.)* I guess she's too old to live alone.

ANDREW. And she's from Berlin? I'd like to ask her what *she* thinks about Hitler.

AGNES. I'm sure she has opinions about everything. Now can we please get in that water? *(Flo stands to stretch and wipe her face with her apron. Agnes sees Flo is six months pregnant.)*

AGNES. *(Stunned.)* Flo!

FLO. What?

AGNES. You wrote, you didn't say nothing about this.

FLO. About what? Oh, *this?* Put news like this on a postcard for every mailman on the Eastern seaboard to snicker at and pass around?

AGNES. Randolph, congratulations! Mrs. Larry, a grandchild!

MRS. LARRY. Life goes on.

FLO. We're not having a *baby.*

RANDOLPH. We're having twins! *(Flo and Randolph kiss deeply.)*

AGNES. Twins don't run in our family.

RANDOLPH. They do now!

MRS. LARRY. What a man Randolph is. Twins! Twins!

AGNES. Andrew, isn't it wonderful?

ANDREW. *(A grimace.)* Congratulations.

AGNES. Let's go in the water and get a cure for the babies!

FLO. This may be your holiday. This is not our holiday.

AGNES. I want the twins to be healthy. At your age!

FLO. Doctor Stackpole says that I can have as many more children as I want. Woman in Peterborough had a baby at forty-nine. And she never went in the water.

AGNES. Mother and Dad would be so happy.

FLO. Now I suppose you'll want twins. Are we playing? *(Flo rakes in the cards.)*

AGNES. What a happy day! My my. Celebrate.

MRS. LARRY. *(To Andrew:)* So you're Velvet Soap?

AGNES. Yes. The executive offices.

ANDREW. Well, actually, I work *in* the —

MRS. LARRY. I know Velvet Soap. I love the hot bubbly lather it whips up. I depend on Velvet Soap to relax me. *(Sings:)* "I'm forever blowing bubbles."

AGNES. Andrew?

MRS LARRY. "Pretty bubbles in the air."

ANDREW. *(To Mrs. Larry:)* You could be a commercial.

MRS. LARRY. Don't tease me, Mr. Soap Suds. "They fly so high, nearly reach the sky."

RANDOLPH. I tell her that all the time.

ANDREW. Radio would love you.

RANDOLPH. Every time I hear Marlene Dietrich, I say that.

MRS. LARRY. Tell that to Mr. Soap Suds. People who hear me comment on my voice.

ANDREW. What about the ones who see you?

MRS. LARRY. They comment on my legs.

RANDOLPH. *(To Flo:)* Heat! Heat! I feel heat!

AGNES. Andrew, come in the house and change —

ANDREW. I feel safer out —

AGNES. The fire's not going to sweep in that fast.

RANDOLPH. The fire leaps at you like a snake! Hisss! *(Andrew backs away.)*

AGNES. Okay. Okay. Then change over in the woods! When we come out of the water, I'll make lunch. Why do I think it's going to be different? And, Flo, I'm still working as a comptometer operator for Felt and Tarrant Accounting. Thank you very much for asking. *(Agnes goes in the house.)*

RANDOLPH. When are you going to get her to sign the paper?

FLO. I can't —

RANDOLPH. If you want me around —

FLO. Don't make me do that —

MRS. LARRY. *(To Andrew:)* Did you fly up here in a private plane? I see them landing on the lake like little dragonflies.

ANDREW. No, no. No! We took the train up from New York — the East Wind to Boston. I've never been to Boston.

MRS. LARRY. One if by land! Two if by sea!

ANDREW. Paul Revere!

MRS. LARRY. The Midnight *Ride* of Paul Revere. *(They laugh lewdly.)*

ANDREW. This is my first time in New England.

MRS. LARRY. Live free or die.

ANDREW. Pardon?

MRS. LARRY. Live free or die is the state motto of New Hampshire. It's the only thing I like about New Hampshire. If I was a state, that would be my motto.

AGNES. *(Off.)* Flo?

FLO. A minute. Let our guest learn about the history of New Hampshire.

RANDOLPH. *(Mouths to Flo:)* I like him. I like him. *(Agnes pokes her head out the window.)*

AGNES. Flo, why are all my things here in the house? My Navajo Indian blanket. You didn't try to rescue my things out of my room?

FLO. It is no longer your room. That is now the twins' room.

AGNES. Seeing as how they haven't been born yet, I don't think they'll mind. How could you not protect my things? I'd protect yours.

FLO. You leave here and think we keep your room like a shrine? *(Agnes goes back in.)* Don't dare touch anything on that bed! The dog sleeps there — if he ever comes home — *(Flo and Randolph study Andrew, who is uncomfortable under their scrutiny.)*

FLO. Are you Cuban?

ANDREW. *(Startled.)* No!

FLO. Funny. I always felt Agnes would bring home a Cuban.

MRS. LARRY. Are you sure you're not Cuban? *(Mrs. Larry tickles Andrew, who laughs giddily. Agnes comes out of the house, a robe over her bathing suit, her hair tied in a bandanna. She carries a Navajo blanket and dolls and photos in a box.)*

AGNES. Flo, I'll just put my worthless things in the boat with your priceless valuables. No hard feelings. *(Agnes shows Andrew a photo.)* See me and my dog, Desdemona! The sweetest dog. She's buried right over there.

RANDOLPH. Not anymore. Didn't an elk appear out of the blue last April and dig up Desdemona and eat her!

FLO. True. You had to laugh. This big elk with this itty bitty white fluffy thing sticking out of its mouth. *(Flo laughs and laughs. Agnes pauses and counts to ten. Then she smiles.)*

AGNES. All right. First one in's — Andrew, come on! *(A drum starts beating.)*

ANDREW. Is that Indians?

FLO. Indians around Squamsquam *or* Winnipesaukee? Never!

AGNES. Hello? *(The drum gets louder. Flo runs into Randolph's arms.)*

FLO. Omigod. Omigod.

RANDOLPH. Don't be frightened! I'm here. Who goes!

ANDREW. *(Alarmed.)* Agnes —

AGNES. Hello? *(A charred woman and man appear. They are The Witnesses. Witness #1, a woman, carries a large burnt sack over her shoulder. Witness #2, a man, carries an Old Testament.)*

WITNESS #1. The Lord has a day of vengeance!

FLO. Oh God, it's those Jehovahs. Get away! Scoot!

WITNESS #2. The champion of Zion has a time of retribution!

FLO. We have no money.

WITNESS #1. Edom's torrents will be turned to pitch.

FLO. Take back your pies if that's what you came for. *(Flo hands them a stack of burnt pies. They refuse.)*

RANDOLPH. Those are my pies!

WITNESS #2. And its soil to brimstone.

FLO. We are not being baptized.

WITNESS #1. The land will become blazing pitch.

RANDOLPH. They won't take no for an answer. When I'm elected —

FLO. We are not being baptized!

WITNESS #2. It is the end of the world!

FLO. We don't have time for the end of the world. We're very busy today.

WITNESS #1. We're trying to save you!

WITNESS #2. Jehovah only has room in his flock for one hundred and forty-four thousand to go to heaven.

FLO. And you suddenly have an opening?

WITNESS #1. Get in that lake and let us immerse you —

WITNESS #2. Be one of the elect!

RANDOLPH. Elect? When I'm elected, I'm having you banned

from the entire state of New Hampshire. Maybe Vermont will know what to do with you.

WITNESS #1. There is no government but the government of Jehovah!

WITNESS #2. There's only two classes of people. The elect and the sheep.

WITNESS #1. Join us.

WITNESS #2. Join us.

WITNESS #1. The world is ending!

WITNESS #2. You have a chance to be saved.

FLO. We don't choose to be saved. Look, you make a darned nice rhubarb pie but as far as eternity goes — *au revoir! (Flo pushes Witness #1 violently off the deck down onto the ground. Agnes runs to the fallen Jehovah.)*

RANDOLPH. You tell 'em, Flo! What's the difference between a Model T Ford and a Jehovah Witness? You can close the door on a Model T! *(Agnes gives Witness #1 a glass of water.)*

WITNESS #2. If you don't want to save yourself —

FLO. We have much better things to do! Go away.

WITNESS #1. Then what about your things?

AGNES. Our things?

WITNESS #2. What about us saving your things? *(The Witnesses pick through the boxes.)*

RANDOLPH. What's this about our things?

WITNESS #1. The world is ending.

WITNESS #2. We're saved.

WITNESS #1. We're safe for eternity.

WITNESS #2. You're not. *(Witness #2 tosses the Bible down like a threat. Witness picks up the leopard-skin coat.)*

WITNESS #1. It's a shame to have these nice things vanish.

MRS. LARRY. Don't touch my coat — *(Mrs. Larry reaches for her coat. Witness #1 tosses it to Witness #2.)*

WITNESS #2. We'll take these things off your hands and save them!

WITNESS #1. Let me wear this leopard coat for one thousand years.

MRS. LARRY. Never! *(Witness #1 puts on the fur coat. Witness #2 opens Agnes' suitcase.)*

AGNES. That's my suitcase! Put that down!

WITNESS #2. If you love your things, give them to us. *(Witness #1 holds up one of Agnes' glasses.)*

WITNESS #1. Don't let these beautiful glasses be annihilated!

AGNES. Put that glass down!

WITNESS #2. Or else they will vanish like all of you!

RANDOLPH. I'm not afraid of fire and I'm not afraid of you! *(Randolph picks up his baseball bat and wields it. Witness #1 pulls a rifle out of her sack. She cocks and aims it. Randolph hides behind Andrew.)*

WITNESS #1. Jehovah is on our side!

RANDOLPH. Andrew! Help me!

ANDREW. I'm just a visitor! Hey, if the world is ending, take what you want! I'll buy a copy of *Watchtower.* I'll take a subscription!

FLO. You're not Jehovahs! Jehovahs are good people! You're thieves pretending to be Jehovahs! *(Flo, Randolph, Agnes and Andrew shrink back in terror as Witness #1 waves her gun. Witness #2 loads the sack with loot.)*

WITNESS #1. When the Lord Jesus is revealed from heaven with his mighty angels in blazing fire —

WITNESS #2. Then he will mete out punishment to those who refuse to acknowledge God and who will not obey the gospel of our lord Jesus Christ. Nice Victrola. *(Witness #2 picks up the Victrola.)*

WITNESS #1. They will suffer the penalty of eternal destruction, cut off from the presence of the Lord and the splendor of his might —

WITNESS #2. — when on the great day — TODAY! — he comes to reveal his glory among his own and his majesty among all believers —

WITNESS #1 and #2. WHO ARE US AND NOT YOU! *(The Witnesses run off through the trees, their arms and sack filled with loot.)*

FLO. Police! Police!

MRS. LARRY. My coat! *(Flo grabs a pitchfork leaning against the house.)*

AGNES. Flo! The twins! Be careful!

FLO. If you think I'm sitting on my duff while those thieves take away our life! *(Flo runs after them.)*

MRS. LARRY. My coat! *(Mrs. Larry runs after Flo. Agnes screams in rage. Agnes picks up the baseball bat and runs off after them in pursuit.)*

RANDOLPH. That's my bat! *(Randolph bursts into tears. To Andrew:)* When I get elected my first step is to put all those Jehovahs in prison forever. They'll pay for this! *(Randolph runs off after the others. Andrew, alone, screams in frustration.)*

ANDREW. Get me out of here! Get in the water. Get the cure. Then take me back to Manhattan, that dear old dirty town. *(Andrew yanks off his jacket, his shirt, his shoes in frustration. He pulls off his pants and folds them neatly on the rowboat. He picks up his swimming trunks as Uncle Ambrose wanders on. He is in his seventies and very sporty. He looks like a derelict Fred Astaire.)*

AMBROSE. You the soap executive?

ANDREW. I'm in the executive offices of the Monitor — are you another one of those Jehovahs?

AMBROSE. You play bridge?

ANDREW. No, they've all gone off that way. Let me change and I'll be right — *(Andrew goes behind the rowboat to change.)*

AMBROSE. They won't like you. You play Monopoly?

ANDREW. No!

AMBROSE. They'll hate you. Monopoly. Bridge. Monopoly. Bridge. Charades. It's hell.

ANDREW. Go away!

AMBROSE. You like murder mysteries?

ANDREW. No!

AMBROSE. They come in with their murder mystery books. I read the end and put the name of the murderer right in the front of the book. That stopped them reading murder mysteries. I'm Uncle Ambrose. Did Agnes tell you about me?

ANDREW. She told me not to give you a drink.

AMBROSE. I'm allergic. Do you have a drink? I see it right in your pocket. Let me wet my whistle. You need a friend. Get on my good side. The others hate you. *(Andrew emerges from behind the rowboat in his bathing suit and singlet. Andrew gives Ambrose his flask out of his pocket. Ambrose drinks as Andrew takes off his socks.)*

ANDREW. Leave something in there!

AMBROSE. You got more packed away in your other pocket. Am

I right or am I right? I'm right. Have a sip. *(Andrew takes out his second flask. They drink.)*

ANDREW. Where do you tend bar?

AMBROSE. At the moment, I'm playing bridge.

ANDREW. Where?

AMBROSE. Here. I'm the dummy. I'm always the dummy. But I'm not the dummy for long. I'm planning my future. There's a cure in the water today. I went in. Prayed to the Blessed Mother for a business associate to show up. What do you know? He shows up.

ANDREW. Who?

AMBROSE. You.

ANDREW. You prayed for me to show up?

AMBROSE. So Agnes finally landed herself a fella. Does she come across?

ANDREW. That's no uncle's business.

AMBROSE. You going to marry her?

ANDREW. *(Indignant.)* No!

AMBROSE. You're a free agent?

ANDREW. You bet I am.

AMBROSE. Good! Then let's talk future. Do you have a future?

ANDREW. I got a future.

AMBROSE. I have a proposition.

ANDREW. I'm just up here for a trip to the country — for the cure in the water. Let me have the flask —

AMBROSE. Forget the cure. You're looking at big dollars.

ANDREW. Big dollars! Sure. Monopoly dollars. Look at this mud hole. All worthless around here.

AMBROSE. They'll tell you it's Lake Squamsquam, but it's going to be Lake Hollywood.

ANDREW. Lake Hollywood?

AMBROSE. One day I was walking along the road you just come up when a yellow Bugatti roadster stops. Very sporty. And in it alone behind the wheel sat Spencer Tracy.

ANDREW. The movie star — was *here?*

AMBROSE. The very same. Asked me if I knew of a lonely motor court he could rent. I said, "Are you Spencer Tracy, the movie star?" And he yelled at me: "I am Dr. Denton and I am a dentist and I am looking for a secluded cabin." I said, "The Oak Birch

Inn over to Alton Bay has nice rooms." But Spencer Tracy the movie star was looking for a hideout. I told him I had a cabin right on the lake. A boathouse. He got out of his yellow car and came right up here where we are.

ANDREW. *(Amazed.)* Here? I love Spencer Tracy!

AMBROSE. I took Spencer Tracy who I called Dr. Denton into the cabin. He saw the tub. He said, "I'll take it." He gave me one hundred dollars.

ANDREW. A hundred dollars! For what?

AMBROSE. In the trunk of his yellow Bugatti roadster, he had packed two cases of twenty-five-year-old Scotch whiskey. He told me to carry the Scotch very careful into the cabin. When I come back, he had took off his clothes, folded them neat on the rocker and was sitting bare-ass in the galvanized tub. He said, "Open me a bottle." I did. He began drinking right from it.

ANDREW. *(Thrilled.)* No!

AMBROSE. I asked Spencer Tracy if he wanted a sandwich. "My name is Dr. Denton!" I said, "Dr. Denton, if I could move the tub you could see Lake Squamsquam." He asked me to draw the curtains till the room was dark and not tell anyone in the world where he was, to come in once a day and pour water over him to clean him off and always keep a bottle of Scotch opened and in reach.

ANDREW. Did he want anything else?

AMBROSE. "Oblivion." That's what he said. "You can buy anything in the world except oblivion. You bring me oblivion and I'll treat you right."

ANDREW. *(Quiet.)* Spencer Tracy feels that way too?

AMBROSE. And that's what I did for a week. Sat right outside here — heard him screaming out "No No No." I'd give him another bottle of Scotch.

ANDREW. I scream out "No No" too but I'm no Spencer Tracy.

AMBROSE. You too? I've been screaming out "No No No" since I was born.

ANDREW and AMBROSE. No No No! *(It echoes across the lake: "No No No!")*

AMBROSE. This is when I got my idea! To build a string of cabins here on the lake.

ANDREW. You own the land? *(Ambrose takes an old map out of*

*his coat pocket and gives it to Andrew.)*
AMBROSE.  From here to way over there.
ANDREW.  All that?
AMBROSE.  If Spencer Tracy can show up here, there must be other movie stars who want to flee the hustle, the bustle, the glamour, the drama, the hotsy and the totsy of movie stardom. I made up a list of famous names who might like my services. Clark Gable after making *Gone with the Wind* for example might like to disappear and have a new name for a while. Ginger Rogers busting up with Fred Astaire might want to get over her grief and vanish. "You can get anything in this world except oblivion."
ANDREW.  Spencer Tracy said that.
AMBROSE.  Oblivion? I finally have something to sell.
ANDREW.  Something to sell ... *(Andrew studies the map.)*
AMBROSE.  You sell soap? We can sell oblivion. Lake Hollywood will be the code word for oblivion.
ANDREW.  Wait. How would these movie stars find out about it?
AMBROSE.  Word of mouth started by Spencer Tracy.
ANDREW.  Did he like it? How long did he stay? Was he satisfied?
AMBROSE.  A week went by and on the seventh day he stumbled out of the cabin, dressed. He tossed me another hundred dollars and he drove away in the yellow Bugatti roadster.
ANDREW.  Did you see him again?
AMBROSE.  Yep. Over in Alton Bay on the screen of the movie theater at the Oak Birch Inn where he was playing Father Flanagan of *Boys Town* for which part I believe he was awarded the prize known as the Oscar.
ANDREW.  The others. Flo? Randolph? Are they all in on this? What do they think?
AMBROSE.  They don't know. They were at a week-long bridge tournament at the Mount Washington Inn. Nobody knows. Only you. I prayed today. I been waiting for you.
ANDREW.  It doesn't have to be movie stars. There's people in the soap industry who'd like to go off on a bender.
AMBROSE.  You know customers? Send them up!
ANDREW.  My boss. Granville Sonnenstrum. The president of the Monitor and Merrimac Soap Company. He embezzled money out of the pension fund to cover bets at the racetrack.

AMBROSE. Did they catch him?

ANDREW. They caught him. He's in prison. He'd love it here.

AMBROSE. Send him up!

ANDREW. God, I'd love it here. A week in a galvanized tub, drinking.

AMBROSE. Check in right now.

ANDREW. I don't have the hundred dollars.

AMBROSE. You're an executive.

ANDREW. I'm not an executive! I work *in* the exec — I got fired. Agnes doesn't know. She thinks I'm on vacation. I loved the soap industry. They threw me out. I'm dead in the soap industry.

AMBROSE. It's even better! You're a free man.

ANDREW. Free? I tried to run away this week to enlist. I'm too old. I have a heart murmur. We're going to get into this war in Europe and I'm not going to be part of it. I was too young for the last war. I'd like to be part of something.

AMBROSE. Be a part of this.

ANDREW. When the smoke clears, I bet it's beautiful.

AMBROSE. I was like you. I always hated it here for having nothing. Spencer Tracy made me love it here. I know one day he'll come back and bring the world with him. All paying a hundred jaboffoes a week! *(The shimmering chord. Just for a moment.)*

ANDREW. To build a colony of cabins on the shores of Lake Hollywood. My God.

AMBROSE. A whole *community* of identical cabins, all around the lake, crammed chock-a-block with movie stars and soap executives looking for oblivion.

ANDREW. And charge them thousands!

AMBROSE. And charge them thousands! Are you on board? I need expert advice. Fifty-fifty?

ANDREW. Forty-nine forty-nine. Two percent for Spencer Tracy.

AMBROSE. Only fair.

ANDREW. Only fair. *(They clink flasks and drink.)*

AMBROSE. That's the kind of thinking I like. *(Andrew is hypnotized by the map. Ambrose takes the flask and drifts off, unnoticed.)*

ANDREW. Maybe it's all turning. This is why I was brought up here. For this. Lake Hollywood. Get in on the ground floor of oblivion. *(To us:)* I see what to do. Not just here, but all across

America, all around the world, the Howard Johnson's of — Nothingness! Lake Hollywood! I just needed the big break, the right magnet to bring my life together! Those big buck friends who ditched me like a leper, they'll be lining up with buckets of cash to invest in this. Lake Hollywood. Go back to New York, get the money and then scoot back here! Uncle Ambrose, it's perfect! *(Andrew turns, looking for Ambrose.)* Ambrose? Ambrose? *(A gunshot! Andrew hides behind the rowboat. A beating drum. Randolph returns in triumph like a pirate, beating the drum, wearing the leopard-skin coat backwards, holding the Witnesses' rifle. Flo follows with her pitchfork and carrying the Victrola. Mrs. Larry follows, toting boxes. Agnes, joyous, follows, carrying the bat and proudly holding the box containing the Czechoslovakian glass.)*

FLO. Randolph! My hero!

RANDOLPH. Back! Back! That's what I said to them. They went back.

FLO. At gunpoint! *(Andrew comes out from behind the rowboat.)*

RANDOLPH. "The world is ending!" Hah!

MRS. LARRY. I would have killed them if they touched one spot of my leopard —

RANDOLPH. Agnes, you're a tiger!

FLO. Randolph, the way you wrested that gun away! What a father you're going to be! I'll tell the twins about this legendary day!

AGNES. And you saved Mother's glasses. *(Agnes shakes the box. The sound of shattered glass.)* Oh. *(Mrs. Larry holds Randolph and Andrew's hands over their heads like champions.)*

MRS. LARRY. I thought the world had no heroes left to rescue us. Today produces two! A two-hero day!

ANDREW. Yes! Rescued!

AGNES. I'll start lunch! *(Agnes kneels on the blanket and takes the prepared ingredients for lunch out of the mesh bag. She puts them in a bowl and begins mixing. Andrew, holding the map, surveys the property.)*

ANDREW. *(To us:)* The cabins will start here! All white clapboard. Not on top of each other. My office will be there in the house! Look at the sunlight flickering on the pine trees. Hear the larks singing —

AGNES. Before I serve the Waldorf salad, Andrew, let's get in that water.

FLO. That water's cold. You don't want Mr. Cheekbones to catch his death.

ANDREW. The water's perfect! Everything's perfect! How cold is it?

AGNES. Not cold at all. Just dunk, for the cure.

MRS. LARRY. You look very able-bodied.

ANDREW. I toss the medicine ball at the beach. *(Andrew falls to the ground and does push-ups.)*

MRS. LARRY. Humor her. I want to see you swim out. I want to see your muscles cut into the water. I want to see your legs kick up foam. I want to see you horizontal. *(Andrew stands and pulls off his singlet.)*

ANDREW. Do I say a Latin prayer or anything?

AGNES. First make a little prayer. Dunk under and say, "Thank you, Mary." That's all.

ANDREW. Thank you Mary. Thank you Mary — *(Agnes and Andrew run into the water and splash. The chord. Shimmering. Agnes pours water over her head and face. Light isolates Agnes.)*

AGNES. *(To us:)* Blessed Mother who was assumed into heaven today by her loving son, let my prayers ascend up with you. Pin my dreams onto your heart so someone important will see them and answer them. It doesn't have to be Jesus. It could be Saint Jude, Patron Saint of Lost Causes. But please? Make it someone who can hear me. Let Andrew love me. *(The chord stops. Lights normal. Agnes and Andrew run back out, laughing, wet, and take towels.)*

ANDREW. I'm cured! For all time!

AGNES. What did you pray for?

ANDREW. Lake Hollywood International.

AGNES. What?

ANDREW. I'm starved! Let's eat! *(Agnes kneels on the blanket to prepare lunch.)*

AGNES. The Waldorf salad invented at the exclusive Waldorf-Astoria Hotel is apples and walnuts and celery cut up in mayonnaise and placed very gently on a bed of iceberg.

MRS. LARRY. Is the iceberg a little wilted?

AGNES. Wilted iceberg is better than no iceberg. Now it's done. But we'll let the salad settle for a few moments to allow the flavors to disperse. While we're waiting, Andrew, as a bread-and-butter gift to all of you, has brought a highly sought-after, very valuable

Monitor and Merrimac Executive Sampler Pack. *(Agnes spills out the Sampler Pack.)* If you're lucky enough to get into the Fred Allen radio show which Velvet sponsors, this is what every audience member gets. Bars and jars.

MRS. LARRY. My. Bars and jars.

FLO. Velvet soap? Used it. Scratched for a week.

AGNES. Then you should use the Velvet Perfumed Skin Softener. Claudette Colbert swears by it. Isn't that right, Andrew? *(Andrew is lost in the map.)*

ANDREW. *(Distracted.)* Yes. Yes.

FLO. Lard is good enough for me.

AGNES. We've gone to the show and met Fred Allen!

FLO. Fred Allen? Too snide.

AGNES. Oh no! He shook my hand. He smiled. Fred's guest that week was Mae West.

MRS. LARRY. Now *she* is funny.

AGNES. Every word out of her mouth is so dirty! "Come up and see me sometime." You want to wash her mouth out with Velvet Soap. I think the salad's ready! Hold out your plates!

MRS. LARRY. I'd like to try this Executive Sampler Pack. To get inside tips from the soap industry — to make sure I'm using the soap in the right way.

AGNES. Mrs. Larry, you don't need lessons for a bar of soap. *(Mrs. Larry goes to the pump and begins pumping slowly.)*

MRS. LARRY. I want to smell like Velvet. I want to make our guest feel at home. *(Mrs. Larry very slowly unwraps the bar of soap. She feels the water.)* The sun heats the water. Will someone help me with my halter? *(Andrew, tripping over the pies, runs to Mrs. Larry who sits by the pump. Andrew undoes the back of her halter. Andrew washes her back very slowly. Agnes is in a rage.)*

MRS. LARRY. Is this the right way?

ANDREW. I think we're doing it right. I'm doing everything right!

MRS. LARRY. So sticky! Come in the water — *(Mrs. Larry goes slowly off into the water. Andrew starts to follow.)*

ANDREW. Agnes, you're the greatest pal. I'm going to give you a share. Wait for me! *(Andrew runs into the water and is gone.)*

RANDOLPH. Wait for me!

FLO. Not in the lake! Don't get soap in the lake. *(Randolph follows and is gone.)* Randolph! Do not get your bandages wet! Agnes, don't stare. Let them have their fun. *(We hear their laughter.)* Isn't Mrs. Larry a pistol?

AGNES. Why are you being so mean to me?

FLO. About Andrew? He's free, white and more than twenty-one. The look of him. So sure of himself. Perfect for her.

AGNES. I see the way Hitler works. He invades little countries, takes what he wants. Siccing that German strudel onto him —

FLO. She's not from Germany.

AGNES. She's from Berlin.

FLO. Berlin, New Hampshire.

AGNES. She's from that Berlin and she's flouncing around like Marlene Dietrich?

FLO. Have sympathy for a widow who's looking for a husband.

AGNES. Let her look somewhere else!

FLO. She behaves and talks that way to make herself interesting.

AGNES. That phony! Maybe she thinks it's interesting.

FLO. This Andrew thinks it's interesting.

AGNES. *(Calls.)* Andrew! *(The echo across the lake: "Andrew!")*

FLO. Don't. I went swimming this morning and I prayed "Dear Mother of God, on this feast of your Assumption, find a husband for Mrs. Larry. Put a cure in my life. Get her out of my house." The Blessed Mother heard my prayer. She sent Andrew.

AGNES. You think that's how he got up here?

FLO. The Blessed Mother put the idea into your head.

AGNES. I put my own idea in my own head.

FLO. You're interested in him for yourself?

AGNES. Why do you think he's here?

FLO. Are you older than he is?

AGNES. Yes! Two years.

FLO. Not good. Someone your own age.

AGNES. I'm too old for Andrew? What about you and Shirley Temple in pants?

FLO. Randolph shaves twice a week. He's mature in outlook. He's obsessed by politics.

AGNES. Why are you throwing snake oil in my path?

FLO. Oh Agnes, marriage isn't for you.

36

AGNES. Then what is for me? I'm not like you. I don't have any broken water pumps to get fixed.

FLO. Hands off Randolph!

AGNES. Believe you me, I don't want Randolph. I want somebody near my own age. You tell me you're having a baby —

FLO. Two babies.

AGNES. *Two* babies. My insides break, Flo.

FLO. Whatever I have, you want.

AGNES. That's right. Water. Light. Air. Food. Happiness. All those strange and unusual things. Flo, I'm so lonely. I meet Andrew. I get him to be my friend. I get him to maybe like me enough to come up here and you do this to me.

FLO. Then get in that water and start praying for somebody else. Andrew is already taken. The Blessed Mother will find you somebody else.

AGNES. I thought I had somebody.

FLO. Andrew's not for you. Let this dime-a-dozen soap salesman invite her to New York. Get her out of my hair. I want to be with Randolph. I love Randolph. I love him. I love him. I love him. *(Flo bursts into tears.)*

AGNES. What's wrong?

FLO. I'm not — I'm not so sure she's his mother.

AGNES. Flo!

FLO. Little clues here. Little clues there. He said he was an orphan down from Maine. Mrs. Larry shows up two days before the wedding. She moves in.

AGNES. She just showed up?

FLO. She had no place to go. I take her in. But things happen between them that make me think — every afternoon they sleep in the same bed. Naps they call it! Naps!

AGNES. Ask detectives!

FLO. I had Marty Quinn ask people in Berlin. Nobody knows her. They both showed up from Maine about four years ago. I have no proof. Get her out of this house.

AGNES. What does she want?

FLO. I'll tell you my worst fear. I think she wants — she wants to steal my babies! Oh God. *(The wind blows. The sky turns red.)*

AGNES. Steal the twins?

FLO.  And sell them! She's always telling me about rich people in big cities wanting to buy babies. She's always saying I'm too old to have babies. I'm not too old! There's a woman in Peterborough — *(Flo clutches Agnes.)* I'm frightened of her —

AGNES.  Oh, Flo. *(The wind changes. The sky is normal.)*

FLO.  I don't dare tell Randolph. Look at him out there! He loves her. She loves him. But you've saved my life. You are the best sister. It's your postcard.

AGNES.  My postcard?

FLO.  Ever since she read your postcard about you bringing up the soap executive, she's been a different person. Her mind's been clicking away.

AGNES.  He just works in the exec —

FLO.  Let her leave with Andrew. Think of someone else for a change. Let me have my babies and my Randolph in peace. Do this for me.

AGNES.  Flo — *(Flo reaches in a box and takes money out of a book.)*

FLO.  I'll give you fifty dollars.

AGNES.  For what?

FLO.  For your share in the house. The real-estate man came by. Chester Babcock said the house was worth upwards of two hundred dollars but I have to put in electricity. A phone. Yes, Nellie Cluff be damned. Indoor plumbing. Randolph is going to open up an appliance store in Wolfeboro. In the winter he can walk right across the lake to work. I'm changing the name of the house to Twins Point which is also going to be the name of the hardware — not to mention appliance store. All the latest in MixMasters and chainsaws and —

AGNES.  Why do you need to buy me out?

FLO.  Because we don't want you dropping in and out at your whim, bringing up men, sashaying around with apples in the salad. I'm nipping that in the bud. *(The low rumbling noise. The Man appears and moves slowly towards Agnes.)*

AGNES.  You think I'm sashaying around?

FLO.  I don't know what you're doing.

AGNES.  Can I ever come back?

FLO.  You can come visit the way a regular loving polite friend would visit by making an appointment, and, if it's not convenient, there's always the Oak Birch Inn.

AGNES. Where am I supposed to go? This is my home.

FLO. You should've thought of that when you sailed that Good Ship Lollipop down to New York City.

AGNES. The World's Fair was showing the future. I wanted to see what it looked like.

FLO. And now you know. I'll tell you what. Fifty dollars *plus* the credenza. I'll throw in the credenza. We'll ship it down to New York.

AGNES. Fifty dollars *and* the credenza?

FLO. Chester Babcock — and there's nobody honester — said it was fair, fair, fair. You and Mother always polishing that albatross. She'd be happy you have it.

AGNES. Where am I going to put it? I live in a room. *(A siren blasts in the distance and keeps repeating. The low rumble continues.)*

FLO. Is that the all clear? My God. The wind's changed. I think everything's going to be all right. Is it twenty-two years since Mother and Father died? Poor Mother and Father. They missed out on so much. Will you take my offer?

THE MAN. "Come on and hear — "

FLO. Going once.

THE MAN. "Come on and hear."

FLO. Going twice.

AGNES. What difference does it make? *(Agnes takes the money.)*

FLO. I forgot. *(Flo reaches in the box and takes out a legal document and pen. Flo holds them out to Agnes.)* Randolph is a stickler for making things legal. *(Agnes signs the paper. Flo takes it.)*

FLO. *(Calls.)* Randolph! You've been in that water long enough! I've done what you want! She said yes! Yes! Yes! *(The echo across the lake: "Yes Yes!". Flo takes boxes back into the house.)*

THE MAN. "They can play a bugle call like you never heard before." *(Agnes walks towards him slowly.)*

AGNES. "So natural that you want to go to war." *(Agnes sits. The Man sits beside her.)*

THE MAN. Get in the car. I know you want a ride. Get in. Red leather. Smell the red leather. *(The Man puts his hand up Agnes' sleeve. She does not move. Randolph runs out of the water, screaming with joy.)*

RANDOLPH. All clear! It's the all clear! We're safe! *(Randolph puts the record on the Victrola: "The World is Waiting for the Sunrise." Flo runs out of the house, waving the paper.)*

FLO. My house is MINE!

RANDOLPH. Did she sign the paper? *(Randolph kisses Flo.)*

FLO. Twins Point is safe! The Jehovahs are defeated! The world is not ending! The world is beginning! Everything back in the house!

RANDOLPH. Agnes, I got to apologize to you. I never liked you very much but you're the greatest sister-in-law in the world. I never seen my wife so happy. I never seen my mom so happy. I just want to keep everybody happy. When I run for office, that's going to be my slogan! Everybody happy! *(Randolph and Flo carry boxes back in the house. Andrew and Mrs. Larry come out of the water.)*

ANDREW. Agnes, Mrs. Larry is coming to New York! Won't that be great!

RANDOLPH. *(Calls out.)* Bring everything in the house!

ANDREW. There's that room available just next to you.

MRS. LARRY. It's my dream to go to New York and be captured by King Kong who takes me to the top of the Empire State Building with planes flying past, shooting at me as he rips my clothes off.

ANDREW. New York is going to love you. *(Flo comes out of the house.)*

FLO. What did I just hear? New York! *(Flo kisses Andrew. The sound of two cars pulling up in the near distance. Horns beep.)*

FLO. *(Calls.)* Is that Marty Quinn? Hi, Marty! Who's that following you? Park the Packard there by the barn!

RANDOLPH. By the barn.

FLO. Not there!

RANDOLPH. Not there!

FLO. There, that's right!

RANDOLPH. That's right!

FLO. Randolph, Agnes is taking the credenza to New York. Boys, bring it over to the barn and strap it to the top of the Packard.

RANDOLPH. Good. I always hated that credenza.

FLO. *(Calling.)* Is that you, Charlie Killian? Did you see Agnes is here! Yes! What a night! All clear! Thank God! *(Flo goes off. Andrew and Randolph pick up the credenza, Randolph using his wrists.)*

40

RANDOLPH. I've often wondered what it would be like having a dad to talk to, to tuck me in at night. I told God I'd believe in him again if he gave me my father back. *(They are off. The sound of the car driving off as Flo comes back with the car keys.)*

FLO. Bye, Marty! Agnes, wave goodbye to Marty and Charlie Killian. *(Agnes waves vaguely. Flo takes the record off.)* Agnes, I'm throwing in the Packard. Take that ancient piece of tin and sell it to the highest bidder! Time we got a new car! Mrs. Larry, I believe that's your suitcase. Everything's new around Twins Point. Agnes and Andrew and Mrs. Larry and the credenza, all of you off to New York! *(Flo hurls Mrs. Larry's suitcase at her. Mrs. Larry picks up her suitcase.)*

ANDREW. I don't drive!

MRS. LARRY. I drive!

FLO. You better get an early start. I don't want you on the road in the dark. *(To Agnes:)* Didn't Mother love that credenza? She loved it more than she loved us. *(Flo goes into the house, happily. The Man still strokes Agnes' arm.)*

THE MAN. "Up to the man who is the leader of the band." *(The Man strokes Agnes' arm. Ambrose staggers on, carrying Andrew's flask.)*

AMBROSE. Don't go in the water without me! There's a cure in the water today. Don't go in without me!

AGNES. Oh, Uncle Ambrose — *(Agnes stands. The Man retreats. Ambrose comes to Agnes. He smiles.)*

AMBROSE. Agnes? I love you.

AGNES. Are you drinking? *(Ambrose falls over. Quiet.)*

AGNES. Ambrose?

THE MAN. You led me on. You led me on. I'm waiting. I'm always waiting. *(The Man puts a peppermint drop on his tongue.)* "Come on along ... " *(The Man goes. Agnes screams. Mrs. Larry runs out of the house to Ambrose. She kneels.)*

MRS. LARRY. He's dead. *(Flo and Randolph come on.)*

FLO. What's happened? *(Flo and Randolph run to Ambrose.)* You can smell the whiskey on him.

RANDOLPH. He's dead.

MRS. LARRY. Death? Death? Not today. No death today. Please! No death today! This is my day! *(Andrew comes out, jaunty.)*

ANDREW. The credenza's strapped onto the roof! *(Andrew sees*

41

*Ambrose stretched out.)* Ambrose? *(Agnes holds out the flask.)*

AGNES. I asked you not to. *(All eyes turn on Andrew.)*

ANDREW. What's he doing? Ambrose? *(Andrew nudges Ambrose. He nudges Ambrose again. He backs away.)*

ANDREW. I didn't do nothing!

FLO. You killed him!

AGNES. I begged you.

ANDREW. I gave him one drink —

AGNES. I asked you not to.

ANDREW. He's a sad man — Ambrose!

FLO. Ambrose sad? He's the happiest — Ambrose! Please? Come back —

RANDOLPH. There's a cure in the water.

FLO. There's cures in the water, not miracles! He's gone.

RANDOLPH. He's gone.

AGNES. He's gone. *(Andrew kneels over Ambrose.)*

ANDREW. Ambrose! Get up! We have to talk about construction costs! Capitalization! Ambrose? Lake Hollywood! Spencer Tracy! *(Andrew stands and pulls on his pants.)* Maybe there's a bus I could catch back —

FLO. And leave us with the body! Pick him up. I can't lift him. Get him to the hospital in Wolfeboro.

RANDOLPH. He doesn't need the hospital. He needs the funeral parlor.

FLO. Get him out of here! Don't mark my babies! *(Flo has a contraction. To the babies:)* Settle down, my little twins. Everything's all right at Twins Point. Look the other way — *(Flo turns her body away.)*

AGNES. Help me, Andrew.

ANDREW. Call an ambulance. Call the police — no phone.

AGNES. We'll drive him to the funeral parlor. Bring the car around.

ANDREW. I don't drive.

AGNES. I'll get the car. *(Agnes goes. Randolph bursts into tears and falls on Ambrose's body.)*

FLO. See what you've done? Ambrose meant the world to Randolph. The father Randolph never —

ANDREW. I'm sorry —

RANDOLPH. You kill my uncle and you say, "I'm sorry"?

FLO. Stop crying. Don't let the twins hear their father crying. Be a man! You're an emperor!

RANDOLPH. *(Weeping.)* When I'm elected — when I'm elected — *(The sound of Agnes trying to start the car.)*

MRS. LARRY. Randolph, Andrew is taking me to New York — *(Mrs. Larry runs to Andrew and kisses him fiercely. Andrew kisses her passionately. Randolph pulls at her.)*

RANDOLPH. Are you leaving?

ANDREW. Yes! She's leaving with me! I have to possess something great!

RANDOLPH. Not my mom!

MRS. LARRY. Sweet Randolph. Finally the wheel of life stops at me. Life is my lover!

ANDREW. And the name of life is Andrew!

MRS. LARRY. Goodbye, Randolph. I wish you the best.

RANDOLPH. You can't leave me! Listen to me! I've got the house. The house is ours.

MRS. LARRY. Then sell it.

FLO. It's my house. It's in my name.

RANDOLPH. Not in New Hampshire where the husband is boss!

FLO. Don't steal my house. Where will the twins go?

RANDOLPH. I did it. What we came for!

MRS. LARRY. Bigger fish have sailed into my net. I see skyscrapers. I see silver towers of steel and glass jutting into the incandescent sky!

RANDOLPH. But, Mother —

MRS. LARRY. You can't woo me with that meaningless word.

FLO. Are you his mother?

RANDOLPH. Of course she is. Aren't you? Aren't you?

MRS. LARRY. I don't remember.

FLO. You don't remember!

RANDOLPH. You don't remember?

FLO. Who is she! Who are you! Mrs. Larry! Who are you? Are you going to steal my babies?

MRS. LARRY. Steal your babies?

FLO. You're going to steal my babies and sell them!

MRS. LARRY. To who? Who'd want your babies? You are so

amusing.

RANDOLPH. Are you leaving with him?

MRS. LARRY. Life is ... a soap bubble. I have to grasp the day.

RANDOLPH. No! No! No!

MRS. LARRY. Randolph, be calm. Hush. Listen to words I leave you with. Words of comfort. And not only to Randolph, but — *(Mrs. Larry turns out to us and talks to us like a regular American:)* — to you too. I am a human being. I talk to you because I recognize that you are all human beings too. Most of you. Not you. Not you. But the rest of you. So much death and unhappiness in this world. All of it is totally unnecessary. Death and unhappiness and poverty are emotions for little people. You know what kills the world? Helping these little people. The little guy. *(She spits.)* The little guy is a little guy because he wants to be a little guy. He does not want to be a human being. He needs to be a dog, waiting for some superior being to toss him a crumb. Do not do it! Let him starve. The meek shall inherit the earth? Hah! I used to be a little person. For years, I looked down in the gutter, picking over the rhinestones of charity. Then I looked up and saw the diamonds of Capitalism hanging over me. I reached up. The Supreme Being told me who I am. Yes, that glowing diamond, that sacred trust, is Me. I am a supreme being. Each of us. All supreme beings! No little people here. Except for you and you. Let's applaud for that hard diamond of ourselves. Me. Me. Me. *(Mrs. Larry takes a postcard from the pocket of her fur coat and kisses it.)* The day Agnes' postcard came, my life began. Andrew is on the side of the angels. An executive. Together we will have the life it is my destiny as a human being to have. When they brought Randolph home this morning just as dawn was stretching out its rosy fingers, the smoke billowed up out of the burning trees and formed for one miraculous moment a dollar sign. One perfect apparition. Right up there in the sky, shimmering over Lake Squamsquam. I bowed to my God. I knew I was safe. *(The sound of the car turning over. And over. Mrs. Larry turns back in to Randolph and resumes her German accent.)*

RANDOLPH. Let me come with you.

FLO. *(To Randolph:)* Don't go. Please don't go!

MRS. LARRY. Randolph, life is for the strong! Charades! Stand up! *(Mrs. Larry points to her leg bone, then thumps her chest.)*

RANDOLPH. Bone? Heart? Bone-a-heart? Bonaparte! *(Mrs. Larry nods yes and flexes her arm muscle and then leans to the side.)* Muscle. Lean. Muscle. Lean — Mussolini!

MRS. LARRY. Yes! Remember the mighty! *(Agnes returns.)*

AGNES. The car is dead. I'm going to row Ambrose over to Wolfeboro.

ANDREW. Row across the entire lake? *(Agnes drags the rowboat from the lawn up to the deck. No one offers to help.)*

AGNES. Andrew, help me row Ambrose over to the funeral parlor. Then you can go back to New York with whoever you want. Will someone help me lift him?

ANDREW. You die in New York, you get on the subway. You die in New York, you call a taxi. *(Andrew and Agnes lift Ambrose into the rowboat. Agnes sits in the stern of the boat, Ambrose's head in her lap.)*

ANDREW. Mrs. Larry, I'll be right back. I feel such courage with you.

MRS. LARRY. I am here, waiting for you like the sunrise.

ANDREW. You are wonderbar. *(Andrew gets in the rowboat and begins rowing. The chord: shimmering. The lights fade on all but Agnes and Andrew. Mrs. Larry, Flo and Randolph wave goodbye and retreat in darkness.)*

MRS. LARRY. Go, my darling. Row the dead to the land of the dead. I wait for you in the world of tomorrow. The land of enchantment. The weak are always jealous of the strong. The pursuit of happiness.

RANDOLPH. Napoleon Bonaparte.

MRS. LARRY. *E pluribus unum.*

RANDOLPH. Mussolini.

FLO. Twins Point.

MRS. LARRY. In God We Trust. *(Sings:)* "I'm forever blowing bubbles."

RANDOLPH. Adolf Hitler. Superman. Attila the Hun. King Charlemagne the Great.

FLO. Hush, my babies. Dead man gone. Everything fine. *(Flo, Randolph, Mrs. Larry are gone.)*

# Scene 3

*Andrew rows across the lake. Sounds of water. Silence. Then:*

AGNES. I'm sorry I ever asked you up. Sorry I ever wasted all those days going to that horrible beach with your horrible friends. I pretended. No more, no more. I'm a fool. Cooking dinners for you. Pretending I like your friends. That beach. I don't care anymore. You can go back to New York tonight. I came up to get my cure in the water. I got it all right. Another year of being perfectly healthy. A nice long long long life.

ANDREW. Do you follow me?

AGNES. Once.

ANDREW. Where?

AGNES. I saw you coming out of the apartment going to the subway and I followed you — to watch you walk. The second time you went to get a haircut and I watched through the window like I was waiting for a bus. *(Agnes recoils from Andrew with real horror.)*

ANDREW. What are you looking at me like that?

AGNES. I saw this movie which is also a book about a poor boy trying to make good who's in love with the beautiful nice rich girl who can give him everything. Except he's got this poor homely girl pregnant who'll only hold him back so he takes her out on a lake and he kills her. *American Tragedy.* That's the name. I should've known that was my story.

ANDREW. But there's no rich beautiful girl in love with me.

AGNES. I'm the other one.

ANDREW. You may be poor. You're not homely. You're not pregnant.

AGNES. I saw you with the Cuban girl taking her once up to your apartment. She was beautiful. She had expensive shoes.

ANDREW. Anna O'Brien? Cuban?

AGNES. O'Brien? She looked Cuban.

ANDREW. What is it with your family and Cubans?

AGNES. Is she wild? I think of Cubans as wild.

46

ANDREW. No. Well, a little bit.

AGNES. Is it serious with her?

ANDREW. Yes. No! This makes me very uncomfortable.

AGNES. What does she do?

ANDREW. What anybody does. A dancer at the Capitol Theater.

AGNES. A Rockette?

ANDREW. That's the Music Hall.

AGNES. But she's in the line?

ANDREW. She's very short. She's the last one.

AGNES. She's too short for you.

ANDREW. You *do* follow me.

AGNES. You brought her up to the apartment. I was getting my mail. I hid behind the curtain in the lobby. You looked embarrassed to be bringing her in to the elevator.

ANDREW. It's a free country.

AGNES. I got to tell you this even though I'll never see you again. The way she dressed. The way she walked. She will not be good for your career. You work in the executive offices. You have a world *(Boston accent:)* caaaaved out for you — I'm saying caaaved — my Boston accent comes back — carved — I could be good for the career you're caaaaving — I can't stop saying caaaaved — I'd be good for your career. I could cook for your bosses. I read that tall men are presidents of railroads — all kinds of companies.

ANDREW. I'm not that tall.

AGNES. You're tall enough to be a vice president. I don't want you throwing your life away on some cheap — Andrew, I may be a virgin. I may be older than you. I may have bowlegs. I may not like my teeth. I may have grey hair. But I'm not cheap. And Mrs. Larry is from Berlin, New Hampshire, not Berlin, Germany, just for your future information.

ANDREW. Berlin, New Hampshire? She talks German.

AGNES. A German shepherd could talk her kind of German. "Live free or die." Oh, Ambrose. Poor Uncle Ambrose. *(Andrew stops rowing.)*

ANDREW. Agnes.

AGNES. Keep on rowing.

ANDREW. I don't have a career. I don't work at the executive offices of Monitor and Merrimac Soap Company anymore. I got fired.

AGNES. Since when?

ANDREW. Three weeks now.

AGNES. You didn't tell me?

ANDREW. I got my pride.

AGNES. Is that why you brought Anna O'Brien up to your room? To tell her?

ANDREW. What do you think I am? No! I didn't tell anybody! Who am I going to tell? It's a mess. My boss embezzled the pension fund. He tried to pin it on me.

AGNES. Granville Sonnenstrum!

ANDREW. There was talk *I* was going to be the fall guy.

AGNES. No!

ANDREW. Oh yes — but I got cleared. But I'm dead in the world of soap. I went to the Army two weeks ago to sign up.

AGNES. Andrew!

ANDREW. I got a heart murmur.

AGNES. Get in the water! The cure —

ANDREW. *And* flat feet, so even if there is a war I got no part in it no matter how many cures are in that water. I got no future in the future. I'm the only one being caaved —

AGNES. Don't make fun.

ANDREW. I'm not making fun.

AGNES. A heart murmur? Should you be rowing?

ANDREW. I'm not a cripple. *(He rows furiously, then stops)* I also got something else to tell you.

AGNES. Oh God.

ANDREW. I can't swim. That's why I don't like lakes. You got to swim in lakes.

AGNES. I seen you swim. In the ocean.

ANDREW. You don't have to swim in the ocean. The salt water carries you. I just bob along. The salt water buoys you up. I just bob along.

AGNES. I never liked Granville Sonnenstrum from the time you brought him out with us to Long Beach. I didn't care if he was your boss. While you were at the store buying beer and cold cuts he got fresh with me in the car. I said this man knows I'm your girl and he's doing this to his friend. I know I'm not your girl but I'm more your girl than I ever was his girl. Granville Sonnenstrum was a weasel.

ANDREW. Why didn't you tell me?

AGNES. I could tell he was a weasel. Anybody could. It was none of my business. You loved your precious Granville Sonnenstrum. I'd rather not have a job at all than have Granville Sonnenstrum for a boss.

ANDREW. He's in prison.

AGNES. Good. He drank too much. You all drink too much. *(She looks down at Ambrose. She covers his head with a blanket.)*

ANDREW. What else don't you like in my life?

AGNES. Go to a gypsy tearoom. I'm no fortune teller.

ANDREW. Who else is a weasel?

AGNES. Mrs. Larry.

ANDREW. She's not in my life.

AGNES. She isn't?

ANDREW. I don't want her in my life. What am I doing? I don't trust anything in my life. I don't know how to make a decision.

AGNES. So don't make a decision.

ANDREW. I did. Before I came up here. I'm leaving New York.

AGNES. When?

ANDREW. The end of the month.

AGNES. Going where?

ANDREW. San Diego.

AGNES. The Pacific Ocean.

ANDREW. I'll try another ocean. I got no future in this one. Agnes, I'm afraid. Don't go using this against me.

AGNES. Who would I tell?

ANDREW. I once told a secret to my brother and he turned me in to my parents.

AGNES. You have a brother?

ANDREW. You're not going to meet him. Ever. I hate families. I hate the country. *(He rows.)* You thought I was handsome? *(Agnes nods yes.)* You think I got a future? *(Agnes nods yes.)* I'm not real smart.

AGNES. Who is?

ANDREW. I got no education.

AGNES. Who does?

ANDREW. I don't have anything to offer a company.

AGNES. You're tall. You're more decent than you'll ever know.

ANDREW. Marry me?

AGNES. What?

ANDREW. Even though I got no money. Well, I got a gold tooth.

AGNES. Marry you?

ANDREW. Maybe asking you in a rowboat with an uncle I just killed is not the best place, but I don't seem to have any sense of when is the right time. What is the right place? Rent a carriage in Central Park and propose to you? Is that what you want? *(Andrew kneels.)* We'll go back to New York and I'll rent a carriage with a white horse and we'll go for a ride around the park and I'll ask you to marry me over and over until you say yes.

AGNES. What about Anna O'Brien?

ANDREW. She said no.

AGNES. *(After a pause.)* I don't want to get married. I don't want anybody around me. I just want to be left alone. It's all over for me. I don't want anything in my life. I make up all these things about life and follow them and it's always a dead end. I got no fingerprints. I could be a criminal. I don't have any shadow. I am not meant to have a life. I don't want to get married. Thank you for asking. Keep rowing. Go back to New York. Go to your ocean. I don't know where I'll go. I'll go to Philadelphia. I'll go — I don't know where — keep rowing. *(Ambrose sits up.)*

AMBROSE. Would you say yes?

AGNES. Ambrose!

AMBROSE. You're not going to get any better offers.

ANDREW. I didn't kill you!

AMBROSE. You got a drink? A hair of the dog!

AGNES. Uncle Ambrose! Row back! Let them know! Row back!

ANDREW. I don't have any more liquor!

AGNES. Row back!

AMBROSE. Never turn back! There's a cure in the water. I can't die. Not today.

ANDREW. Don't tip the boat over! I can't swim!

AGNES. Row back! Tell them you're alive!

AMBROSE. No! Tell them I died. I never want to play bridge or monopoly or charades again. You want to come with me, Agnes?

AGNES. No!

ANDREW. *(Terrified.)* Don't tip the boat over!

AMBROSE. All you ever say is no. The hell with you! You want to come with me? What's your name?

ANDREW. Andrew!

AMBROSE. Andrew! I'm going to California to find Spencer Tracy.

AGNES. Spencer Tracy?

ANDREW. Spencer Tracy was here.

AGNES. You're all crazy. Get me out of here!

ANDREW. I want to marry you!

AGNES. No!

AMBROSE. Agnes, don't say no too often. Don't be like me. I said no over and over and now I'm hoping it's not too late. Say yes, Agnes. Don't be like me. I'm finally starting. Better late than never.

AGNES. You can't walk on water — *(The shimmering chord. Ambrose steps overboard onto the water.)*

AMBROSE. Yes, I can. I'm hoping there's a cure in this water for my life! *(Ambrose walks off on the surface of the rippling water, smiling.)*

AGNES. Uncle Ambrose! Uncle Ambrose? *(Ambrose is gone. The boat rocks back and forth. Andrew grabs Agnes by the arm.)*

ANDREW. Marry me, Agnes? Marry me? Or we'll die!

AGNES. No! *(The rumbling noise begins. The Man and The Young Girl, in her swimsuit, appear at opposite sides of the stage.)*

THE MAN. You want a ride? Get in. Get in. Get in. *(The Young Girl walks powerlessly toward The Man. Agnes, terrified, reaches out to Andrew.)*

AGNES. Andrew! *(The Young Girl and The Man vanish. Agnes and Andrew clutch each other in the boat.)*

### END OF ACT ONE

# Entr'acte

*The Young Girl appears in her bathing suit.*

THE YOUNG GIRL. *(To us:)* Water comes next to air as a life necessity; it should be the best the earth affords. New Hampshire, the Granite State, has water power in abundance. *(Andrew and Agnes call out of the wings:)*

ANDREW. Honey, we're in New York.

THE YOUNG GIRL. New York?

AGNES. It's forty years later and we're in New York.

THE YOUNG GIRL. Forty years later?

ANDREW. We're in New York City. *(Agnes and Andrew, followed by two actors in the company, come onstage. Agnes and Andrew's clothes are speckled with white. They speak to us.)*

AGNES. Our lives take place in three blocks.

ANDREW. Three blocks.

AGNES. One block is when we're very young. Then the second block, which is most of our lives.

ANDREW. Which you just saw.

AGNES. And then the third block when we're very old. *(The two actors produce flour sifters, which they hold over Andrew and Agnes. The two actors sift flour down onto Andrew and Agnes.)*

ANDREW. Really old.

AGNES. When that wrinkled face we don't recognize in the clear mirror is our own face. We think we're still in the second block.

ANDREW. I still look the same to me ...

THE YOUNG GIRL. You look very old. *(Andrew snarls at her and goes, followed by the two actors.)*

AGNES. But face it, Andrew and I are in the third block —

THE YOUNG GIRL. The last block?

AGNES. Look at you — still in that first block — dreaming dreaming ... *(The Man appears out of the dark. The rumbling noise.)*

THE MAN.  Get in. You need a ride. Get in. *(The Young Girl backs away. Agnes protects her. The Man circles them. The Young Girl runs away. The Man circles again. Agnes is terrified. The Man goes.)*

# ACT TWO

## Scene 1

*The hall of a tenement flat in the West Fifties in New York City. Water drips down into buckets.*

AGNES.  Andrew? Andrew?  Are you up there? Are you down there? *(A woman appears in the dark.)*
MRS. GARCIA.  You don't have shoes on. *(Agnes wheels around. It's an Hispanic neighbor, Mrs. Garcia.)*
AGNES.  He's back.
MRS. GARCIA.  Who's back? *(Another neighbor, Mr. Ede, appears, angry.)*
MR. EDE.  Then send him to 2-D. The water pipe's broken. Water down the walls. Water on the floor. I told him yesterday. Nothing.
AGNES.  Where's Andrew?
MR. EDE.  I'm looking for him. You said he was back. He's not in the basement. He's not on the roof.
MRS. GARCIA.  This is not the right day to —
MR. EDE.  His job is to be here when we need him. Didn't I leave a big-enough tip at Christmas? Is this the punishment? *(Mrs. Garcia whispers to Mr. Ede.)* I don't care where she's going. I need my water pipe fixed. Water out of the ceiling. Water into the floor. Send him down to 2-D. *(Mr. Ede goes.)*
MRS. GARCIA.  I thought you left already.
AGNES.  I haven't.
MRS. GARCIA.  If you need any help today —

53

AGNES. I don't!

MRS. GARCIA. Hospitals run on a tight —

AGNES. Everybody trying to rush me. I don't need any hospital steamroller. I want Andrew! *(The phone rings. Agnes runs into the apartment. The deck is now the living room. The remnants of the last act are still visible. The small living room is dominated by the credenza, which is much too big for the small room. It's tall and square. The lower half is lined with drawers. The upper half is glass cabinets, meant to display dishes. All manner of notes, snapshots, holy cards and receipts are stuck in its glass doors. She picks up the phone.)* Andrew? *(Hildegarde, forty, appears in the distance.)*

HILDEGARDE. Mother, we are running late.

AGNES. I woke up. He's not here. But the man is. The man came back —

HILDEGARDE. Who's not here?

AGNES. Your father's not here.

HILDEGARDE. Daddy's not there?

AGNES. Did he call you?

HILDEGARDE. He didn't call. George, did my father —

AGNES. I drove Andrew away. He knew the man was back and he left —

HILDEGARDE. What man? *(George, forties, appears.)*

GEORGE. What's happening? Hello, Agnes —

AGNES. I thought maybe he called you — I don't know where he went.

GEORGE. Did he leave a note?

HILDEGARDE. Mother, look and see if Father left a note.

AGNES. Hang on. A note a note — *(Agnes puts down the phone and looks up at the credenza. She takes various pieces of paper off the glass and holds them close to her eyes. A flurry of other papers fall to the floor.)*

AGNES. Moo Goo Gai Pan. Prawns with chili sauce. China Supreme. Throw that away. Phone bill turn off. Pay by 1982. We're talking. We must've paid it —

HILDEGARDE. Mother — *(Calls off.) Monica!* Are you dressed?

AGNES. Novena novena to Saint — who? Lucy — patron of eyesight. "Dear Saint Lucy, protect my eyes." Too late too late. Raffle ticket raffle ticket. Oh! Ten cents off Brillo pads. Fifty cents off

Ajax cleaner. Fifty cents! Save that.

HILDEGARDE and GEORGE. Mother, is there a note —

AGNES. Snapshot. Randolph before he died. So young. Snapshot. Oh no! Flo. *(Kisses it.)* My darling sister. A widow with those twins. Look at the twins. The way they turned out — is this child Hildegarde? Little Hildegarde. *(In phone:)* Look at the tassel on your graduation hat swinging right over your nose —

HILDEGARDE. Is there milk?

AGNES. Of course there's milk.

HILDEGARDE. Ma. Look in the fridge. *(Agnes puts the phone down and goes behind the credenza.)*

AGNES. I'm looking — don't hang up — milk. Milk. Why does she want milk? *(Agnes returns.)* No milk. Remember to buy milk *(In phone:)* No milk.

HILDEGARDE. He went out to buy milk. *(Monica appears, fifteen.)*

MONICA. Grandma? Should I call the police? Missing persons? Maybe Grandpa's dead.

HILDEGARDE. Monica! Shut up. Mother. We're on our way. Do you hear me? Do not panic! Do not lose it. Everything's going to be okay. *(Hildegarde hangs up. They go into dark.)*

AGNES. Andrew!

## Scene 2

*The stable.*

*Andrew, age eighty, carrying a plastic bag with a quart of milk in it, walks into a stable on Fifty-Second Street and Twelfth Avenue. Horses whinnying.*

ANDREW. Hello? Hello? *(Vinnie enters, carrying a bucket and a horse-grooming brush.)*

VINNIE. Hello?

ANDREW. Hello? How much this cost? A carriage ride in one of these carriages.

VINNIE. We don't do pickups out of here. You wait outside the Plaza Hotel.

ANDREW. I live up the street. I seen the stable here all these years. I always meant to come in.

VINNIE. Half an hour around the park is —

ANDREW. Not around the park.

VINNIE. A wedding? Church to reception? I don't go over the bridge.

ANDREW. Just up the street.

VINNIE. Up what street?

ANDREW. This street. We live up the street. I always seen this stable here — all these carriages that go around the park. I can even hear the horses. My wife's going to the hospital. I thought I'd take her in a carriage.

VINNIE. What hospital?

ANDREW. The one up the street.

VINNIE. Saint Clare's? That's just up the street.

ANDREW. Saint Clare's up the street.

VINNIE. It's one block. You walk up the street.

ANDREW. I don't want to walk up the street and I'm wondering how much it costs.

VINNIE. Thirty-four dollars half an hour around the park.

ANDREW. I'm not asking to go thirty-four dollars half an hour around the park. I'm asking up the street for two minutes.

VINNIE. You take the horse out, that's automatic thirty-four —

ANDREW. You got to go up the street anyway to go to the Plaza. Right?

VINNIE. Right.

ANDREW. You drop us off at the hospital.

VINNIE. You take the horse out, that's automatic thirty-four —

ANDREW. Look. I promised my wife if she'd marry me, I'd take her on a carriage ride.

VINNIE. You're getting married?

ANDREW. We're married. Now we're going to Saint Clare's.

VINNIE. To the hospital?

ANDREW. Not the hospital. A carriage ride. I'm just thinking while I'm buying the milk, I did not keep my promise.

VINNIE. When did you make this promise?

ANDREW. I'm not a calendar. What? Maybe forty years? Fifty.

VINNIE. You think she still remembers?

ANDREW. I'm the one who remembers. Look. To go from here up the street where you got to go anyway is no thirty-four dollars. That's five dollars.

VINNIE. The horse goes out. You get in. Thirty-four dollars.

ANDREW. That's robbery.

VINNIE. That's automatic.

ANDREW. I'm no tourist. I'm born here all my life.

VINNIE. Thirty-four dollars outside the Plaza. Sorry.

ANDREW. I hope you make a promise someday. *(Andrew goes.)*

## Scene 3

*The apartment.*

*The phone rings. Agnes picks it up. Hildegarde appears in light.*

AGNES. Hello!

HILDEGARDE. We are at the gas station at the mouth of the Lincoln Tunnel because George naturally forgot to put more than two drops of gas into the car. We are currently in the self-serve lane where George can't even fit the nozzle into the — *(To George:)* What do you mean cash? Insert the credit card. You forgot the credit — *(Hildegarde loses the connection and goes into dark.)*

AGNES. Hello? Hello? Don't go! *(The rumbling noise starts. Agnes crouches behind a chair and holds up her hands.)*

AGNES. Stay away stay away stay away stay away — *(Andrew comes in, carrying the bag with the milk.)*

ANDREW. Me stay away?

AGNES. The bad man. He knows I'm here.

ANDREW. I got you milk. *(Andrew goes behind the credenza to put*

57

*the milk away and comes out.)* Are you packed?

AGNES. He found me. *(Andrew looks at the papers on the floor.)*

ANDREW. What happened? A tornado? *(Andrew picks up the papers.)*

AGNES. How did he find me?

ANDREW. Hospitals run on a tight schedule.

AGNES. I'm sweating. I'm on fire.

ANDREW. Tell this to the doctor.

AGNES. No! The doctor can't help me. It's him. He found me! He still keeps running after me.

ANDREW. The doctor ran after you?

AGNES. Not the doctor! The bad man.

ANDREW. What bad man?

AGNES. The bad man running after me. He found me! I don't need a doctor. I need to jump in the lake!

ANDREW. Jump in what lake? *(The phone rings.)*

AGNES. Don't! If I can jump in the lake I'm safe! I want to go to New Hampshire!

ANDREW. Maybe it's Hildegarde.

AGNES. I don't want to talk to Hildegarde.

ANDREW. She's driving in special —

AGNES. Everybody rushing in to speed me up. If I can get to New Hampshire — get in the lake — get the cure —

ANDREW. It's nowhere near the fifteenth of August. August is a whole other month.

AGNES. We go up and wait! And one day, it'll be the fifteenth of August and I can go in the water and I'll be safe. I won't need any doctors. That's what's wrong with me. I haven't been in the lake for years and years —

ANDREW. Lake Hollywood.

AGNES. What's Lake Hollywood? Lake Squamsquam. My lake. *(The phone keeps ringing. Andrew reaches for it.)* Leave it!

ANDREW. Maybe it's the doctor.

AGNES. What more could the doctor say?

ANDREW. That he made a mistake. That you don't have to go.

AGNES. Dr. Damon don't make mistakes. You see all those degrees on his wall. Andrew — the man found me! *(The phone keeps ringing.)* He found me — how did find me?

ANDREW. Who found you?

AGNES. I'll tell you. Let me tell you. *(He's alarmed by her intensity. She tries to tell. She turns away. The phone still rings. Andrew picks it up. Hildegarde appears.)*

ANDREW. Hello?

HILDEGARDE. Daddy? Where the hell have you been?

ANDREW. I got milk —

HILDEGARDE. You go for milk, you call me. These are very delicate times. We're just out of the tunnel, heading up Tenth Avenue. Don't close up the suitcase. I got a bed jacket for her. Lace.

ANDREW. *(To Agnes:)* She's got a jacket for you.

AGNES. I give up. You want him to get me. I knew this day would come. He's here.

HILDEGARDE. I'm bringing you my suitcase.

ANDREW. She don't need a suitcase. She's packed. You packed?

AGNES. I'm packed.

ANDREW. She's packed.

HILDEGARDE. Unpack. I'm bringing you a suitcase. They take better care of you if they see you got a nice —

ANDREW. She's bringing you a suitcase.

HILDEGARDE. Where's the suitcase? I told you to put the suitcase in the car — watch out for that — *(They lose the connection. Dark. Dial tone.)*

ANDREW. We got suitcases — hello? Hello? *(Andrew hangs up the phone. Agnes puts on her coat over her housecoat.)*

AGNES. If we left now, we could leave a note for them to meet us there.

ANDREW. They're driving in special to drive you up. They pay tolls. *(Agnes puts on a hat and picks up her suitcase.)*

AGNES. I don't want to ride with them.

ANDREW. They drove in from New Jersey.

AGNES. It's a block away.

ANDREW. It's a long block.

AGNES. Once they get me in there, I'll be flat on my back full of tubes and nurses and needles and knives. I want to walk with you.

ANDREW. Dr. Damon said you'll only be there a couple of days.

AGNES. Maybe he says. All I'll be doing is resting so if we walk I'll get tired. I want to walk with you. I want him to see I'm not alone. I want him to see I got protection.

ANDREW. They're coming any minute —

AGNES. *(Shows a note.)* I wrote a note!

ANDREW. "We went already."

AGNES. Stick it on the door. They'll go right to the hospital. Please? Don't the prisoner get one last wish? I want to walk with you.

ANDREW. You didn't sign it.

AGNES. They're going to know it's from us. Why waste ink? *(She picks up her suitcase. They go out in the hall. Agnes puts the note in the door. Andrew starts to close the door. Agnes holds the door.)*

AGNES. Wait. Look at that — *(Agnes goes back in and takes a paint-by-the-numbers oil painting off the wall.)*

ANDREW. I don't have time to fix anything.

AGNES. That streak on the wall. See? The painters had just finished painting and the walls were still wet and we were fighting about something and I got mad at you and threw the grapefruit I was eating at you and you ducked and the grapefruit stuck to the wet wall and slid all the way down to the floor.

ANDREW. That's the streak?

AGNES. The painters were finished so I hung this over it. *(Agnes brings him the painting.)*

ANDREW. What's the picture?

AGNES. You found it in the street.

ANDREW. It's a lake.

AGNES. It looks like New Hampshire.

ANDREW. Lake Hollywood.

AGNES. There's no Lake Hollywood in New Hampshire.

ANDREW. Where you lived.

AGNES. That was Lake Squamsquam off Winnipesaukee.

ANDREW. Why do I think Lake Hollywood?

AGNES. You only went there once. Don't go bringing up that.

ANDREW. I never noticed this. A lake. That's a nice picture. *(She goes back in the apartment and replaces the picture. She looks around the room. She comes out. He closes the door. They start down the corridor. They hear Hildegarde, George and Monica coming in.)*

HILDEGARDE. I have a full life in Cliffside that you want to take me away from —

GEORGE. Your self-esteem clinic is the pits.

60

HILDEGARDE. You know how much self-esteem I got? How about no esteem? And you want to take us to Spokane? *(Agnes looks at Andrew. They go back inside the apartment and lock the door behind them. They stand very quiet. Mrs. Hasselbach, an old woman, appears as Hildegarde raps on her parents' door. Water drips down into buckets.)*

HILDEGARDE. We're here, mama! Knock knock knock! *(To George:)* Whatever you do, you will not mention one word about Spokane — *(Agnes and Andrew stand quiet. Mrs. Hasselbach approaches them.)*

MRS. HASSELBACH. You thinking of giving up your parents' apartment?

HILDEGARDE. No, Mrs. Hasselbach.

MRS. HASSELBACH. I'd love to break through. *(Mr. Ede and Mrs. Garcia appear.)*

MR. EDE. My water pipe's broke.

HILDEGARDE. Mama? You don't suppose anything's happened? Mama? Mrs. Hasselbach? You seen them go?

MRS. HASSELBACH. They're still in there.

MRS. GARCIA. She could've snuck up to the roof.

GEORGE. Hello? Mom? Pop? *(Agnes looks at Andrew.)*

MONICA. Maybe they killed themselves?

HILDEGARDE. Shut up, Monica!

MONICA. You read all the time old people kill themselves.

MRS. HASSELBACH. Plastic bags right over the head.

MR. EDE. The water's spilling like Niagara.

MRS. GARCIA. I saw her this morning headed up to the roof.

HILDEGARDE. Oh my God! Where's my key?

MRS. HASSELBACH. You want me to call the police?

HILDEGARDE. Oh, no — break the door down!

ALL. Knock knock knock. *(Agnes relents.)*

AGNES. Oh. We're here. Knock knock knock. *(Agnes opens the door. Hildegarde, George and Monica come in. The neighbors attempt to follow.)*

HILDEGARDE. Hello, Mama, knock knock knock.

MRS. HASSELBACH. If I knock this wall down I can enlarge — *(Agnes stops the neighbors and pushes them out.)*

AGNES. It's not a convention, Mrs. Hasselbach.

61

MRS. HASSELBACH. We're trying to help —

HILDEGARDE. It's all right, Mrs. Hasselbach —

MR. EDE. My water pipe —

AGNES. Thank you, Mr. Ede. *(Agnes closes the door on the neighbors. Hildegarde hugs Agnes.)*

HILDEGARDE. Why didn't you open? We have had the worst trip in —

GEORGE. Just shut up, Hildegarde —

HILDEGARDE. I left your suitcase right by the door for George to pick up but can he do that?

GEORGE. I said I'm sorry —

MONICA. Hello, Grandma. I'm sorry you're sick.

HILDEGARDE. Your grandmother is not sick. Your grandmother is going in for exploratory. Exploratory is not sick. Exploratory is the good side of prevention. You look wonderful, Mama.

AGNES. I want to go to New Hampshire.

HILDEGARDE. Oh Mama, don't lose it now.

GEORGE. So how you doing, Andrew?

ANDREW. I'm doing fine. *(Andrew turns on the TV. Andrew and George watch.)*

HILDEGARDE. Do we have to have that? *(Andrew turns off the sound. Andrew and George watch the TV. Monica sits, playing with a video game.)*

GEORGE. We parked the car two blocks away. A white Mercedes pulled out just as we came up the block so that's good luck.

HILDEGARDE. A drug dealer. Good luck. Sure.

GEORGE. Any time you're ready to leave, we'll go get the car again.

AGNES. We're just going up the street —

HILDEGARDE. We're going to sit down and rest and let one of us catch my breath. The drive we have had in here — *(Hildegarde sits on the couch. George stands up, disgusted. Hildegarde covers her head.)*

HILDEGARDE. Don't you dare hit me! *(Andrew and Agnes look up, alarmed.)*

GEORGE. I'm going to get a beer. *(George goes behind the credenza.)*

ANDREW. There's milk. You want milk? *(Quiet, to Hildegarde:)*

He hit you?

HILDEGARDE. Dad. Today is not about me.

MONICA. He never hit you.

HILDEGARDE. He will. It's a matter of time. Take his side, Monica. Take his side.

GEORGE. *(Off.)* Anybody want a glass of something?

HILDEGARDE. I would like some water. Put sugar in it.

AGNES. Sugar?

HILDEGARDE. The doctors are doing advanced experimenting on my sugar levels which don't register on any chart.

AGNES. Are you all right?

HILDEGARDE. I should worry you today of all days with any of my petty concerns? *(George returns with a beer and a glass of water.)*

GEORGE. And the winner of the saddest girl in the universe contest is — !

HILDEGARDE. *(Sip.)* You don't seem to understand this is a very emotional day for me.

AGNES. How's your water?

HILDEGARDE. My — oh, this water. Fine. Not as good as Jersey water — but fine. The sugar makes it sweet.

GEORGE. Spokane has got like the best water in the world running right off the mountains. *(Hildegarde puts her glass down firmly.)* I'm sorry.

HILDEGARDE. You had to bring it up.

GEORGE. I'm sorry.

HILDEGARDE. I say, "Don't bring up Spokane." So what do you do? Spokane Spokane Spokane.

GEORGE. I'm sorry.

ANDREW. Spokane?

GEORGE. We're moving to Spokane.

HILDEGARDE. Maybe you are.

ANDREW. You're moving where?

GEORGE. They're opening a new office in Spokane and I got put in charge.

ANDREW. In charge?

AGNES. In Spokane?

HILDEGARDE. George, how do you think they feel about you

63

dragging me off to Spokane?

AGNES. We don't mind.

HILDEGARDE. Don't lie.

AGNES. Where's Spokane?

GEORGE. I thought they were calling me in to fire me.

HILDEGARDE. You know how I find out? A real-estate agent comes to the door to show our house.

GEORGE. I forgot to tell you. I'm sorry.

HILDEGARDE. This stranger says, "You're moving to Spokane."

ANDREW. Congratulations.

GEORGE. Your father knows what to say. A simple congrats —

HILDEGARDE. You men stick together.

AGNES. What's Spokane?

HILDEGARDE. Spokane is beyond Canada.

GEORGE. I thought they were calling me in to fire me.

HILDEGARDE. Spokane don't sound like no promotion to me. Spokane sounds like they're dumping you.

GEORGE. You know what would be a good idea? You don't come to Spokane.

HILDEGARDE. You trying to dump me for one of those Xerox sluts in the Xerox room? Close your ears, Monica. You didn't hear this.

MONICA. *(To us:)* Spokane, in the state of Washington, is the largest city between Seattle and Minneapolis, is 110 miles south of the Canadian border and, with a population of 188,300, is the most populous Northern city in America and that includes Alaska.

HILDEGARDE. Monica's shattered. She doesn't want to go.

MONICA. Fifty-one percent of Spokane is female while forty-eight-point-seven are male. There is no personal income tax in Washington State.

GEORGE. *(Over Monica:)* Sammy Barnett lost his job and he's got more years with the company than me so when they called me in —

MONICA. Eighty-six days of the year in Spokane have clear skies with only nineteen days of the year that temperature is over ninety degrees while thirty-eight of those days will have a temperature of under thirty-two degrees.

HILDEGARDE. *(Over Monica:)* I'm a mind reader to know

Sammy Barnett got fired?

MONICA. Spokane's situation in either the Rocky Mountains or the Cascade Mountains protects it from the damp coastal weather, say, of Seattle, as well as mean winters, say of New York.

HILDEGARDE. Monica, shut up, Monica. You wouldn't tell me? No. I'm always the last to know. What else don't I know? Have you got some Xerox bimbo waiting out in Spokane? Close your ears, Monica. I'm not furniture you move around. He thinks that I'm a credenza. I'm no credenza. I have roots in Cliffside. Monica has roots in Cliffside.

MONICA. The median age in Spokane is thirty-three-point-seven years.

AGNES. Would you like the credenza?

HILDEGARDE. That? Are you kidding?

AGNES. You could take it to Spokane.

HILDEGARDE. Where's your suitcase?

AGNES. There. *(Hildegarde takes Agnes' suitcase.)*

HILDEGARDE. You're not taking a garbage bag —

AGNES. It's my bag —

HILDEGARDE. George, you want them thinking she's an illegal immigrant? Is that what you want? If today was his family he'd be out slaughtering alligators to make fancy suitcases. But *my* family —

AGNES. I like my suitcase.

HILDEGARDE. Don't you have any other suitcases?

ANDREW. In the bedroom closet —

HILDEGARDE. Don't help, George. Just sit there like a blob. *(Hildegarde goes behind the credenza.)*

GEORGE. Andrew, you have a nice voice. Agnes, you have a nice voice. Where did she get her voice from —

HILDEGARDE. *(Off.)* I got it from you. You know all I got from this marriage? This voice. *(George follows. Monica looks at photos on the credenza.)*

AGNES. That credenza was my mother's. Your great-grandmother's.

MONICA. Did I know her?

AGNES. She died in 1918.

MONICA. Were you alive in 1918?

AGNES. I been alive since whenever. Would you like the credenza?

MONICA. No.

AGNES. I see you looking at it.

MONICA. Who's this?

AGNES. My sister's boys. The twins. Your mother's first cousins. They're your second cousins.

MONICA. Mama said twins run in our family.

AGNES. Muffin and Chipper when they were ten.

MONICA. Which one is dead?

AGNES. If that's Muffin, he's dead.

MONICA. And Chipper's in prison?

AGNES. Maybe. We never kept up.

MONICA. Who's this?

AGNES. That's — I can't make it out —

ANDREW. That's Mrs. Larry.

AGNES. How did *she* worm her way onto my credenza?

ANDREW. She was the twins' grandmother.

AGNES. Maybe. Maybe. You kept her here all these years? *(Agnes rips the photo.)*

MONICA. She's my relative!

AGNES. On another side. No family to you.

MONICA. What happened to her?

AGNES. Her skin fell off. Isn't that right?

ANDREW. What are you looking at me for?

AGNES. Did you ever see her again?

ANDREW. She and me got married and had ten children and all of them are millionaires and I have this other life for fun.

MONICA. Can your skin do that? Just fall off?

AGNES. Yes.

MONICA. Just fall off?

AGNES. How old are you?

MONICA. Fifteen.

AGNES. Do you have a man?

MONICA. I got a boyfriend. He's the captain of the swimming team.

AGNES. I mean, a man. A man who chases you.

MONICA. I don't think so.

AGNES. Don't let him chase you. They own you. They never let you go.

ANDREW. What are you talking?

AGNES. They chase you and you hide and they find you. They never stop looking.

ANDREW. Your grandmother's a little upset today.

AGNES. He found me.

MONICA. I'm the only sophomore on the committee of the Fall Festival. The theme is Vietnam and I have a long dress.

ANDREW. You're going to be a good-looking girl.

MONICA. That's not what Mama says. She says I have Daddy's upper lip.

ANDREW. Do you want to go to Spokane?

MONICA. Summer weather is ideal for full enjoyment of the many mountain and lake recreational areas in the vicinity.

AGNES. You sure you wouldn't like the credenza? Going once.

MONICA. No. *(Agnes takes the picture off the wall.)*

AGNES. Would you like this?

MONICA. A lake?

AGNES. The blue part is a real lake. *(Monica takes the picture.)*

ANDREW. Lake Hollywood. *(Hildegarde and George return with about ten old suitcases.)*

HILDEGARDE. The dust! The dust! You two never go anywhere. What are all these suitcases doing here?

ANDREW. I find them out on the street. *(Hildegarde throws the cases down.)*

HILDEGARDE. You are not having other people's suitcases in this house.

ANDREW. People throw good suitcases away.

GEORGE. No! We can use these suitcases.

HILDEGARDE. I hate all these suitcases! I am not moving to Spokane! I am not leaving Cliffside. Other people's suitcases! I will not have you living like this! I want these out in the street now. Father! Get them out of here! Go to Spokane on your own. *(Hildegarde weeps. George and Andrew pick up all the suitcases and go out the front door to keep peace. Agnes starts after Andrew.)*

AGNES. Andrew?

HILDEGARDE. Suppose we were in Spokane. How would you get to the hospital today?

AGNES. I'd walk.

MONICA. Look what Grandma gave me.

HILDEGARDE. Monica is not being rewarded today. *(Hildegarde hands the picture back to Agnes.)*

AGNES. It's just a lake. *(Hildegarde takes Agnes' suitcase and empties the nightgowns out of it onto the floor.)*

HILDEGARDE. You cannot take this nightgown. Or this. Nurses treat you the way you treat your nightgowns. Holes. Holes.

AGNES. I like them —

HILDEGARDE. At least I brought you a bed jacket. Nurses respect bed jackets. Where is the bed jacket ? Authentic lace at the neck.

MONICA. In the suitcase at home.

HILDEGARDE. Which George made me forget. If it was his family, he'd hock the house to buy gold bed jackets. What's in this suitcase? Mice have been living in this suitcase. Can you help, Monica? Reach me that suitcase — *(Hildegarde picks up the nightgowns and dumps them into the original suitcase.)*

AGNES. That's the old suitcase.

HILDEGARDE. It's good enough.

AGNES. Would you like the credenza?

HILDEGARDE. Mama, I always hated that credenza.

AGNES. It's got a secret drawer.

MONICA. Where?

AGNES. My mother was always going to show me and then she died. I've looked and looked …

HILDEGARDE. That's creepy.

AGNES. Creepy? My credenza?

HILDEGARDE. Don't be frightened, Ma.

AGNES. I am frightened. The man found me.

HILDEGARDE. Of course you're frightened. We're all frightened. I'm frightened. Moving across the country. You depend on me. You come to Spokane.

AGNES. Don't worry about me.

HILDEGARDE. Oh, it's not you. It's George. When you said Daddy was missing this morning, I thought Daddy walked out. All these men running out the minute the going got tough.

MONICA. Daddy's not running out on you.

HILDEGARDE. How do you know?

MONICA. I asked him. He told me.

HILDEGARDE. You didn't have a real-estate agent showing the house to strangers.

MONICA. He forgot to tell you!

HILDEGARDE. Unless he was going to sell the house out from under me —

AGNES. I don't think George would do that to you.

HILDEGARDE. Your very own sister screwed you out of your very own house. Every time I read about a politician going to New Hampshire to run for president, I think I could be living there on a lake. I'd be happy there. I could be voting in New Hampshire for a president in a primary. I'm so glad I never had sisters.

MONICA. You told me you did have a sister who died.

HILDEGARDE. She was only a baby.

AGNES. *(Quiet.)* That's all.

HILDEGARDE. She didn't even have a name.

MONICA. I'm glad I don't have any family —

HILDEGARDE. You have me.

MONICA. *(Snide.)* Aside from you. *(Silence. Hildegarde cries and falls in Agnes' lap.)*

AGNES. *(Sings:)* "Dear One, the world is waiting for the sunrise."

HILDEGARDE. "Every rose is heavy with dew."

AGNES. That's the Hildegarde I like to see.

HILDEGARDE. I'd like to crawl up here and stay here forever.

AGNES and HILDEGARDE. *(Sing:)*
> The thrush on high
> His sleepy mate is calling
> And my heart is calling you.

*(George and Andrew come back in.)*

GEORGE. The minute I go out of the room she starts singing.

HILDEGARDE. *(Sitting up.)* Now don't try and make up.

GEORGE. Maybe I should stay out of the room more often.

HILDEGARDE. Maybe you should.

ANDREW. Hospitals run on a tight schedule.

HILDEGARDE. Oh Papa, you're always in such a hurry. It's so nice here. My God, we won't always have this chance. *(Pause.)*

GEORGE. That's a rotten thing to say.

HILDEGARDE. Mama, I didn't mean that. This is the truth —

if we go to Spokane, what would I do today?

MONICA. The topography of the land varies from rolling wheat fields to snow-capped mountains.

GEORGE. Just leave Spokane out of it. Look at your father. He's quiet. He's happy. Why don't you take after him?

ANDREW. I'm just thinking today, George.

HILDEGARDE. How you're going to be a bachelor while Mama's away? You think you can trust him on his own? Mrs. Hasselbach has always had that squinty eye of hers on Pop.

AGNES. I think I can trust him.

ANDREW. Of course you can.

HILDEGARDE. You're taking everything so serious today. We're only teasing. Okay, are we all set? Bag. Coat.

ANDREW. Bag. Coat.

AGNES. Bag. Coat.

HILDEGARDE. Papa, Monica has her first date next Saturday. The high school junior prom. Isn't that nice? *(George signals his in-laws not to get involved in this conversation.)*

GEORGE. Maybe we better get started —

MONICA. Mother —

HILDEGARDE. What's he saying — Oh, he doesn't want to talk about Monica. He knows he did wrong.

GEORGE. I did not do wrong.

MONICA. Daddy did not do wrong.

HILDEGARDE. George here goes out and buys her this fantastic evening gown. *(Agnes and Andrew sit down again until this storm passes.)*

MONICA. It's my first prom and I'll remember it forever.

HILDEGARDE. Cut down to here. You're only fifteen. You'll look like a freak.

MONICA. That's what you think I am?

GEORGE. Your father probably did the same thing for you.

HILDEGARDE. He never did.

ANDREW. What wouldn't I do?

HILDEGARDE. My father never bought me a dress even though I did my homework and was such a good girl I could spit seeing the way girls act today and because I simply demand to see my daughter's homework even though you never asked to see one syllable of my homework not once and never said word one to me about my maybe being good enough to go to college and not have my daughter end up like me who married the first man who came along to get out of the house because of the yelling that went on here.

AGNES. We didn't yell.

HILDEGARDE. The two of you didn't yell? Living here was like living in a war zone.

AGNES. It was?

HILDEGARDE. Dishes flying. The insults!

ANDREW. We have to go.

HILDEGARDE. Everything I ran away from, that's all I got. I'm going to get the car. I'll be back in a few minutes.

AGNES. You don't have to —

GEORGE. I'm driving the car.

HILDEGARDE. I will drive my parents to the hospital. As our parents see us *into* the world, so it is my duty to see my parents *out* of this world.

GEORGE. I'll be right back. Be waiting out front. *(George goes.)*

HILDEGARDE. You're not stepping foot in — we'll be right back. Be out front. It's going to be all right. We'll take care of Daddy no matter what happens — you are staying with us while Mama's away. I'm going to move you out to Cliffside until we leave. You start packing your bag —

ANDREW. I don't want to leave here.

HILDEGARDE. Don't be another one of the chorus who argues with me.

ANDREW. I have things to do here.

HILDEGARDE. You never go anywhere.

ANDREW. I could if I wanted to.

MONICA. Grandma, could I bring my class over next Tuesday?

HILDEGARDE. She doesn't want visitors.

AGNES. If I'm alive, sure.

MONICA. It's Career Day. You could talk to them.

HILDEGARDE. What would she tell them?

AGNES. The credenza. I'd tell them about that.

HILDEGARDE. That horrible thing?

AGNES. Are you sure you don't want to take the credenza to Spokane?

HILDEGARDE. No!

ANDREW. Remember when it had rubber tires on it?

HILDEGARDE. Papa, don't *you* go losing it.

ANDREW. To float out onto the lake — the fire —

AGNES. The lake. The man —

HILDEGARDE. Monica — come on. *(Hildegarde goes.)*

MONICA. I got a present for you. *(Monica takes an envelope out of her pocket and gives Agnes a sheet of construction paper with glitter and feathers pasted on it.)*

AGNES. It says "Get well." You made this?

MONICA. I was up all night making it.

AGNES. It's got feathers. Andrew? Look!

ANDREW. What's this?

MONICA. Macaroni pasted with glitter.

AGNES. You got a real gift.

MONICA. I do?

AGNES. Put this in my bag. I'll hang it by my bed.

HILDEGARDE. *(Off.)* Monica! *(Monica runs off.)*

ANDREW. She forgot the lake.

AGNES. It'll take them fifteen minutes. We could walk down the block in fifteen minutes. Please. I don't want to drive with them. I already wrote the note. It's a shame to waste the note.

ANDREW. We'll get a cab.

AGNES. No! I want to walk. Are you tired?

ANDREW. I don't want people thinking I'm a cheapskate.

AGNES. Who? The hospital? Mrs. Hasselbach? Is a bag full of ripped nightgowns too heavy? People know you're no cheapskate. When we first moved here, I said it'll be good. Kids ever sick, you ever sick, hospital is up the block. We can walk. So in forty years, nobody ever gets sick enough to have to go the hospital except me now. So let me get something out of living here forty years. Let me walk to the hospital.

ANDREW. Just don't go throwing it back at me later I made you walk.

AGNES. Do you like the credenza?

ANDREW. I never thought about it. *(Agnes looks around the apartment.)*

ANDREW. You'll be back next week.

72

AGNES. Yeah. Next week. *(Agnes steps into the hall. Andrew follows and starts to close the door. She holds the door.)*

AGNES. Wait. *(She looks once around the apartment.)*

AGNES. All right. *(They step out into the hall. Water drips down into buckets. Mrs. Garcia appears.)*

MRS. GARCIA. Don't let them cut you up. They find a million things wrong with you.

AGNES. Thank you! Thank you! *(Mrs. Garcia removes furniture from the apartment. Mr. Ede appears.)*

MR. EDE. The water pipe is broke.

ANDREW. I'll fix it tomorrow.

MR. EDE. I need it today.

ANDREW. I'm taking a sick day.

MR. EDE. You don't look sick to me.

ANDREW. Tomorrow.

MR. EDE. My dog had what you have and they put him to sleep.

AGNES. Thank you, Mr. Ede. *(Mr. Ede removes furniture from the apartment. Mrs. Hasselbach appears.)*

MRS. HASSELBACH. I saw your daughter and son-in-law were here a few minutes ago. Are they getting divorced?

AGNES. They came in from New Jersey.

MRS. HASSELBACH. Whereabouts in New Jersey? I have relations in New Jersey. There's good parts in New Jersey and there's horrible parts.

AGNES. Nice seeing you, Mrs. Hasselbach.

MRS. HASSELBACH. Are you giving up the apartment? I'd love to break through from my apartment into yours.

ANDREW. We're not giving up the apartment.

MRS. HASSELBACH. I didn't notice any ambulance out front.

AGNES. We didn't call any ambulances, Mrs. Hasselbach. We're walking.

MRS. HASSELBACH. On a day like this you're walking?

ANDREW. Don't let her think I'm a cheapskate.

AGNES. And it's not because he's a cheapskate.

MRS. HASSELBACH. Who's feeding you while she's away?

ANDREW. The Koreans on Ninth Avenue got food.

MRS. HASSELBACH. Bean curd ain't food.

ANDREW. I saw chicken.

MRS. HASSELBACH. Chicken in embalming fluid all the way from Korea is not food. I'll give you chicken. Chicken Hasselbach. Thank God you're finally going in. You look horrible. I'll come visit you if you don't have anything contagious. Good luck. *(Mrs. Hasselbach removes furniture from the apartment. The stage is bare.)*

## Scene 4

*The street.*

*Andrew and Agnes are out on the street. He carries the suit-case.*

AGNES. Feel the sunshine across the street! Look at her up in the window behind the curtain. No matter what happens, don't let Ivy Hasselbach get the credenza! Promise me?

ANDREW. I promise. You wanted to walk, we walk.

AGNES. I wanted to tell you — *(She holds on tight to Andrew's arm.)*

ANDREW. What? What did you want to tell me? *(They walk a few more steps. Agnes stops.)*

AGNES. I wanted to — *(A siren. The sounds of a fire engine roaring by.)*

ANDREW. Do you smell smoke?

AGNES. I got to tell you something!

ANDREW. Tell me. I smell smoke.

AGNES. I don't want to tell you in the street.

ANDREW. Tell me in the hospital. It's not the hospital —

AGNES. I don't want to tell in the hospital. I want to tell you where I'm safe.

ANDREW. We're safe here — the fire — it's over there — not the hospital — *(Wally, nineteen, sets up a table, two chairs and an African mask, and goes.)*

AGNES. All this time I always meant to go in this restaurant.

74

## Scene 5

*The restaurant.*

*They go in the small restaurant. Strange music plays from whatever country this is. Andrew and Agnes sit at the table and look around.*

ANDREW. Medicare pays for your food in the hospital.

AGNES. Look at the pictures.

ANDREW. Volcanoes and spears? You feel safe here?

AGNES. This used to be Chinese. I love Chinese. *(Calls out:)* Hello? Are you still Chinese?

ANDREW. Water? This country serve water? This country got any bread? What do you got to tell me?

AGNES. — what happened to me this morning.

ANDREW. I go out to get milk. I come back. Tornadoes on the floor.

AGNES. He found me. All these years.

ANDREW. Who found you? *(Wally, the waiter, appears. He wears a dashiki and a cap. She looks up at him.)*

AGNES. *(Stunned.)* I know you! It's Wally!

ANDREW. Pantoni!

AGNES. Wally Pantoni.

WALLY. I know you.

AGNES. I can't believe it!

WALLY. I thought I saw you —

ANDREW. You lived in 4B.

AGNES. Can you sit down with us?

WALLY. They don't allow —

ANDREW. You're working here?

WALLY. I forgot your name.

AGNES. Look who our Chinese waiter is!

WALLY. I'm not Chinese. You're the super and his wife.

AGNES. We're remembered!

WALLY. I can't remember your name. You were always fighting —

ANDREW. It's Wally Pantoni in 4B. When did you turn Chinese? You got any rolls? *(Wally puts down menus.)*

WALLY. They don't eat rolls in Abyssinia.

AGNES. This is Abyssinia! Imagine!

WALLY. Can I take your order? They don't like me talking to —

AGNES. How are your wonderful parents?

WALLY. After the divorce —

AGNES. Divorced? The wonderful Pantonis?

ANDREW. Are they Abyssinian?

WALLY. No, we're Greek.

ANDREW. You were always Italian.

WALLY. Pantoninopolos. They changed it to fit in.

AGNES. I thought you fit in.

WALLY. They never did.

ANDREW. I remember the night you were born. The Mets won the World Series.

WALLY. I always watch the World Series for my birthday.

ANDREW. I thought you'd be an athlete.

WALLY. I'm a waiter for now.

AGNES. What do you dream of doing? You hear on the television about the young people today having wonderful dreams.

WALLY. As soon as I get my truck fixed, I'm going to be a furniture mover.

AGNES. What a coincidence! Our daughter's moving to Spokane.

WALLY. We don't do Spokane. We do local for now.

AGNES. Maybe they'll wait for you to go national.

WALLY. You think?

AGNES. You like furniture?

WALLY. I think furniture's a good idea.

AGNES. That's right. A good idea.

ANDREW. What do you eat here? *(Wally points out the menu.)*

WALLY. That's goat.

AGNES. I'll try anything.

ANDREW. I don't want to get sick.

AGNES. I'm on my way to the hospital. That old joke — is it good luck getting hit by an ambulance? It's there to pick you up.

WALLY. *(Calls:)* Two goats!

ANDREW. Only one. We're in a hurry! *(Wally goes.)*

AGNES. The Pantonis divorced!

ANDREW. They were a nice family. So what do you want to tell me?

AGNES. I wish I met your family.

ANDREW. Is that what you dragged me in here to tell me?

AGNES. I'm just thinking this now. You and me walking along Thirty-Fourth Street one day and I see you coming towards me except I'm with you and you say to this man who is your exact double, "Hello, Frank" and the man says, "Hello, Andrew" and you both keep on walking. "Who's that?" And you say, "My brother."

ANDREW. So?

AGNES. Why wouldn't you let me meet him?

ANDREW. What's there to meet?

AGNES. Your brother.

ANDREW. Brothers.

AGNES. You had brothers?

ANDREW. Three of them.

AGNES. Three brothers?

ANDREW. I didn't want you knowing them.

AGNES. Were you embarrassed about me?

ANDREW. After the funeral, we went different ways. This isn't important. What do you want to tell me?

AGNES. Whose funeral?

ANDREW. Nobody's funeral.

AGNES. It's got to be somebody's funeral.

ANDREW. We got to go.

AGNES. You don't bury nobody.

ANDREW. My mother's.

AGNES. I never heard you ever say one word about your mother.

ANDREW. What's there to say?

AGNES. Look! We're in Abyssinia and everybody says everything.

ANDREW. *(With difficulty.)* One Halloween — all us boys —

AGNES. Your three brothers?

ANDREW. We was making a racket, screaming and fighting and

77

my mother said, "If you boys don't stop fighting." Her veins turned blue in her neck — we have to go.

AGNES. No.

ANDREW. My mother — started screaming at us to shut up and then she fell over. "Get up, Mom." All us boys thought she was kidding. "Get up. Halloween. Trick or treat."

AGNES. She fell over?

ANDREW. We gave her a stroke.

AGNES. Dead?

ANDREW. Dead. After the funeral, we all went different ways.

AGNES. Is that why you never drink on Halloween?

ANDREW. I hate fighting.

AGNES. Where was your father?

ANDREW. He died a long time before. The fighting *they* did.

AGNES. You could have told me this.

ANDREW. What's there to tell? What do you want to tell me? *(Wally brings them food.)*

WALLY. One goat! Hot plate! Hot plate! Only kidding. *(She digs in to the food. She likes it.)*

AGNES. You got a girl?

WALLY. I'm seeing a girl who's in transportation.

ANDREW. A stewardess?

WALLY. The subways. She sells tokens and MetroCards.

ANDREW. You must get a discount. Are you serious?

WALLY. Well, I hope we get back together. I think she's got her eye set on somebody better than me.

AGNES. With the right breaks, nobody will be better than you. You'll work out. I feel it. A handsome guy like you. Isn't he handsome! I'm so sorry about your parents. Do you see them?

WALLY. Well, my father moved back to Greece but he got there and his brother had sold the family house from under him so now my father's homeless in Athens.

AGNES. Didn't my sister do the very same thing to me! She lived in our house with her husband Randolph and the two twins until poor Randolph went ice-fishing one night on Lake Squamsquam and didn't the ice crack under him and close over him!

ANDREW. Agnes, Wally doesn't —

AGNES. They found Randolph weeks later still frozen in a block.

And left the twins completely fatherless.

ANDREW. Agnes, forget the twins.

WALLY. My mother's a twin.

AGNES. I thought I saw her in two places at once. Twins! I have enough problems being one person. My nephews were so identical even Flo couldn't tell them apart.

ANDREW. Agnes —

AGNES. And Chipper and Muffin had to be separated at age sixteen because they kept trying to kill each other with hatchets. Can you sit down with us?

WALLY. No. They don't allow us to mingle —

AGNES. So Abyssinia.

ANDREW. We got to go. What's the damage?

AGNES. Andrew, I'm not finished. Goat! Imagine. *(Agnes chews her food. Wally makes out the bill.)*

AGNES. Wally? You ever move a credenza?

WALLY. A what?

ANDREW. Agnes —

AGNES. A credenza's got shelves on the top half behind glass doors to put your good dishes in and you open up the bottom part and it's a desk with a secret drawer to put stuff in and it's almost mahogany.

WALLY. I could move that.

AGNES. He could move that! *(A bell rings. Wally leaves the check and goes. Andrew takes out his wallet. She takes a napkin and writes on it, using Wally's pencil.)*

ANDREW. What are you writing?

AGNES. "To Wally Pantoni, I leave one credenza."

ANDREW. You're not leaving the credenza to Wally Pantoni!

AGNES. I'm not having my credenza end up in any Spokane. Whatever happens to me, let Wally take it away. I want it legal. I don't want whichever one of the twins is alive showing up waving a hatchet saying, "Give me back the credenza." They stole the house from me. That house was mine as much as my sister's! This credenza will make Wally feel proud. Wait till that girl of his gets a gander at the credenza! She'll come running back to him. Wally Pantoni is not going to be anybody's second choice.

ANDREW. Agnes, what's coming over you today?

79

AGNES. She'll see he's no damaged goods.

ANDREW. Who's damaged goods?

AGNES. *(In a breath.)* Me! Me! Me! When I was fifteen, I had a job at McGrath's in Alton Bay helping at the soda fountain and one day after work I walked back home. It was August the fifteenth. I had my bathing suit on under my uniform. I wanted to get in the water because of the cure. I heard a car behind me which was a rare sight on the lake road. I stopped to let it pass. The snazzy convertible stops and this guy opens the door, "Get in. You want a ride?" I never been in a snazzy car. We drove off. Red leather seats. I loved being in that car. I put my legs up on the dashboard. I told him all about the Blessed Mother and the cure in the water. He leaned close. He said I was very interesting. I thanked him. He put his hand on my leg. His hand was very cool. I could see the lake. He pulled off the main road onto the grass. He put his hand up under my uniform and got hold of the strap on my bathing suit. I said this is not the way to the lake. He ripped the strap on my bathing suit and put his face close to me. He stuck out his tongue. It had a white peppermint drop on it. He reached to kiss me. I bit into his face. I flew out of the car. I ran like a deer. I could hear his footsteps behind me. I was at the water's edge. I could taste his blood on my mouth where I bit him. I jumped in the lake and started swimming. He ran along the shore holding his face, yelling, "I'll get you. Wherever you go, I'll get you. You led me on. You led me on." I swam and swam until I saw home and Flo standing by the cabin door, holding a yellow piece of paper which was a telegram from Boston saying our parents had both died of the Spanish flu. "You lead me on." I never told anybody what happened. My sister Flo or Uncle Ambrose or anybody. I'd lay awake for nights, waiting for him to get me. "You led me on." I came to New York to get away. I married you, but he was always there, looking for me. "You led me on." I was always afraid I'd do something famous like be the millionth person to ride on the subway and my name would get in the paper and he'd see it and come get me. "You led me on." All these years I lay low. I never turned him in. I never mentioned him. *(Pause.)* And now I have.

ANDREW. I wish you told me this before.

AGNES. Who'd want damaged goods? I was damaged goods.

ANDREW. Agnes, we have got to get to the hospital. *(Wally comes back.)*

AGNES. Compliments to the chef.

ANDREW. It's the first time I never heard her ask the waiter, "Is it clean?"

AGNES. You got to experiment. *(Agnes puts on her coat.)* We left you a big tip.

WALLY. It's funny working in the old neighborhood. I thought you were all dead.

AGNES. Give us time! *(Andrew pulls her along. They walk out into the street. Wally clears the table, chairs, African mask and goes.)*


# Scene 6


*The street.*


AGNES. The Pantonis divorced! You could knock me over —

ANDREW. I wish George and Hildegarde didn't fight so much.

AGNES. You know what I'm going to tell Monica and her class when she comes on Tuesday? I'm going to tell her she's lucky her parents still fight. Keep on fighting! That's the worst part of getting old. You don't miss the love part, the sex part, the not being able to have kids part. You think that's the part you're gonna miss but you know it's gonna go. No, the one thing I always thought we'd have, you and me, is the fights. God, didn't we toss some beautiful battles? The neighbors hammering on the walls. Not even a hot bath or a cup of tea can make you feel as clean as when I'd finish yelling at you and you'd finish yelling at me. That's the worst part of getting old, I decided. You just don't have the energy to fight.

MAN'S VOICE. Get in.

AGNES. What's that?

MAN'S VOICE. Get in. You want a ride? *(Agnes is terrified. The heart-pounding rumbling noise starts. She grabs onto Andrew. They hear the clip-clop of a horse. Andrew turns. Vinnie appears and stops*

81

*his carriage. [He carries a bench.])*

ANDREW. Hello!

AGNES. He's here. The lake. Let me get in the lake. The lake will save me. *(Agnes tries to run. Andrew holds her.)*

ANDREW. Agnes, stop it. It's a horse and carriage.

VINNIE. Hey, get in!

ANDREW. Thirty-four dollars?

VINNIE. I got to go past there anyway.

ANDREW. But it's just there.

VINNIE. I'll give you once around the block. Free!

ANDREW. Get in.

AGNES. This man —

ANDREW. He works in the stable down on Twelfth Avenue —

VINNIE. Vinnie.

ANDREW. My friend Vinnie.

AGNES. You know him?

ANDREW. Yes — get in — *(Andrew helps Agnes up into the carriage. They step onto the deck and sit on the bench.)*

ANDREW. You're not going to spring any fare jumps on me —

VINNIE. Relax. *(Andrew sits back. Vinnie has his back to us. The carriage moves around the block. The sound of the horse's steps.)*

AGNES. I knew you'd keep your promise.

ANDREW. I don't want him springing any fare jumps —

AGNES. Thank you for that.

ANDREW. This?

AGNES. That. Back there.

ANDREW. The goat or telling you about my family?

AGNES. The goat or my family? It sounds like the punch line to some joke. Who was that old comedian on the radio?

ANDREW. George Burns? Gracie?

AGNES. No.

ANDREW. You liked Jack Benny.

AGNES. I'm thinking — not Edgar Bergen.

ANDREW. Fred Allen?

AGNES. Fred Allen! You read my mind. Remember the old Fred Allen show on the radio about the house blew up and the old man and woman go flying through the sky and she says, "This is the first time we been out together in twenty years." *(The sound of the*

82

*horse's steps fades.)*

ANDREW. Fred Allen was very funny. What did he do to you?

AGNES. Who?

ANDREW. That man.

AGNES. What man?

ANDREW. That man. What did he do to you?

AGNES. Nothing. The Blessed Mother saved me.

ANDREW. Then how are you damaged goods?

AGNES. He must've seen something bad in me that made him stop the car.

ANDREW. "Get in. You want a ride?" That's what he said? *(The rumbling noise starts.)*

AGNES. "Get in. You want a ride." He's here. He's still here. I want to get out — *(Andrew holds her. The rumbling noise fades.)*

ANDREW. Wait. How old was he?

AGNES. Old.

ANDREW. Was he older than you?

AGNES. A lot older than me.

ANDREW. Look how old we are. If you're this old, he must be dead.

AGNES. Dead?

ANDREW. He's dead.

AGNES. Dead? I never thought of this before.

ANDREW. He's dead.

AGNES. He can't get me?

ANDREW. He's dead.

AGNES. I'm safe?

ANDREW. He's dead!

AGNES. *(Amazed.)* My God.

ANDREW. He's not even chasing you in a walker.

AGNES. That car?

ANDREW. Run out of gas.

AGNES. That dirt road?

ANDREW. Paved over.

AGNES. The Jehovah Witnesses?

ANDREW. All on fire.

AGNES. The pine trees?

ANDREW. All burned down.

AGNES. The birch trees?

ANDREW. Long since gone.

AGNES. The house?

ANDREW. All gone. All gone.

AGNES. The lake?

ANDREW. The lake. Only the lake.

AGNES. Only the lake. I'm alone with you. I never been alone. All this. He was there. Hildegarde. Life. He was always there. He's dead? I'm safe! We'll go to New Hampshire. We'll dunk in the lake. We'll get the cure. We'll keep the house. You'll get the right job for a man so tall. A man of your abilities. We'll live forever. This is only temporary.

ANDREW. Temporary.

AGNES. Velvet Soap. Beautiful Velvet Soap. *(Sings:)* "I'm forever blowing bubbles" —

ANDREW. Don't go bringing up Velvet Soap.

AGNES. You were very important. Those executive packs — *(The sound of the horse's steps.)*

ANDREW. Look. There's our house.

AGNES. There's Mrs. Hasselbach — the school — the church — *(She watches them recede.)*

VINNIE. We're here. *(The carriage stops. Andrew and Agnes step down. Vinnie and his carriage go off. Andrew picks up her bag. She takes his arm.)*

AGNES. God, Fred Allen was funny, wasn't he? *(The chord. Shimmering. Transcendent. They step into the dark.)*

**The End**

# PROPERTY LIST

Boxes
Suitcase(s)
Mesh shopping bag containing groceries (AGNES)
Flasks (ANDREW, AMBROSE)
Lit cigarette (MRS. LARRY)
Baseball bat (RANDOLPH, AGNES)
Playing cards (MRS. LARRY)
Blanket (MRS. LARRY, AGNES)
Stack of pies (RANDOLPH)
Glass (AGNES)
Leopard-skin coat (MRS. LARRY, RANDOLPH)
Bottle (MRS. LARRY)
Navajo blanket (AGNES
Dolls (AGNES)
Photos in a box (AGNES)
Large burnt sack (WITNESS #1)
Old Testament (WITNESS #2)
Glass of water (AGNES, GEORGE)
Rifle (WITNESS, #1, RANDOLPH)
Victrola (WITNESS #2, FLO)
Pitchfork (FLO)
Swimming trunks (ANDREW)
Old map (AMBROSE)
Box containing shattered glass (AGNES)
Bowl (AGNES)
Water (AGNES
Towel (AGNES, RANDOLPH)
Packages containing bars and jars of soap (AGNES)
Book (FLO)
Money (FLO)
Legal document (FLO)
Pen (FLO)
Record (RANDOLPH)
Car keys (FLO)
Peppermint drop (THE MAN)
Postcard (MRS. LARRY)

Flour sifters and flour (TWO ACTORS)
Pieces of paper (AGNES)
Photographs (AGNES)
Plastic bag containing a quart of milk (ANDREW)
Bucket (VINNIE)
Horse-grooming brush (VINNIE)
Coat (AGNES)
Hat (AGNES)
Note (AGNES)
Paint-by-the-numbers oil painting (AGNES)
Video game (MONICA)
Beer (GEORGE)
Picture of a lake (AGNES)
Suitcase containing nightgowns (HILDEGARDE)
Envelope containing sheet of construction paper with glitter and
    feathers pasted on it (MONICA)
Table (WALLY)
Two chairs (WALLY)
African mask (WALLY)
Menus (WALLY)
Two plates of food (WALLY)
Check (WALLY)
Pencil (WALLY)
Wallet (ANDREW)
Napkin (AGNES)
Bench (VINNIE)

## SOUND EFFECTS

A sustained single chord
Car speeding by
Wind
Low rumbling sound
"The World is Waiting for the Sunrise" played on a Victrola
Sharp noise
Echo of dialogue in the play
Drum beating
Gunshot
Siren
Cars pulling up
Car horn
Car driving off
Car turning over
Sounds of water
Phone ring
Horses whinnying
Dial tone
Television
Fire engine
Abyssinian music
Bell
Horse's footsteps

# NEW PLAYS

★ **AS BEES IN HONEY DROWN by Douglas Carter Beane.** Winner of the John Gassner Playwriting Award. A hot young novelist finds the subject of his new screenplay in a New York socialite who leads him into the world of *Auntie Mame* and *Breakfast at Tiffany's*, before she takes him for a ride. "A delicious soufflé of a satire … [an] extremely entertaining fable for an age that always chooses image over substance." *–The NY Times* "… A witty assessment of one of the most active and relentless industries in a consumer society … the creation of 'hot' young things, which the media have learned to mass produce with efficiency and zeal." *–The NY Daily News* [3M, 3W, flexible casting] ISBN: 0-8222-1651-5

★ **STUPID KIDS by John C. Russell.** In rapid, highly stylized scenes, the story follows four high-school students as they make their way from first through eighth period and beyond, struggling with the fears, frustrations, and longings peculiar to youth. "In STUPID KIDS … playwright John C. Russell gets the opera of adolescence to a T … The stylized teenspeak of STUPID KIDS … suggests that Mr. Russell may have hidden a tape recorder under a desk in study hall somewhere and then scoured the tapes for good quotations … it is the kids' insular, ceaselessly churning world, a pre-adult world of Doritos [and] libidos, that the playwright seeks to lay bare." *–The NY Times* "STUPID KIDS [is] a sharp-edged … whoosh of teen angst and conformity anguish. It is also very funny." *–NY Newsday* [2M, 2W] ISBN: 0-8222-1698-1

★ **COLLECTED STORIES by Donald Margulies.** From Obie Award-winner Donald Margulies comes a provocative analysis of a student-teacher relationship that turns sour when the protégé becomes a rival. "With his fine ear for detail, Margulies creates an authentic, insular world, and he gives equal weight to the opposing viewpoints of two formidable characters." *–The LA Times* "This is probably Margulies' best play to date …" *–The NY Post* "… always fluid and lively, the play is thick with ideas, like a stock-pot of good stew." *–The Village Voice* [2W] ISBN: 0-8222-1640-X

★ **FREEDOMLAND by Amy Freed.** An overdue showdown between a son and his father sets off fireworks that illuminate the neurosis, rage and anxiety of one family – and of America at the turn of the millennium. "FREEDOMLAND's more obvious links are to *Buried Child* and *Bosoms and Neglect*. Freed, like Guare, is an inspired wordsmith with a gift for surreal touches in situations grounded in familiar and real territory." *–Curtain Up* [3M, 4W] ISBN: 0-8222-1719-8

★ **STOP KISS by Diana Son.** A poignant and funny play about the ways, both sudden and slow, that lives can change irrevocably. "There's so much that is vital and exciting about STOP KISS … you want to embrace this young author and cheer her onto other works … the writing on display here is funny and credible … you also will be charmed by its heartfelt characters and up-to-the-minute humor." *–The NY Daily News* "… irresistibly exciting … a sweet, sad, and enchantingly sincere play." *–The NY Times* [3M, 3W] ISBN: 0-8222-1731-7

★ **THREE DAYS OF RAIN by Richard Greenberg.** The sins of fathers and mothers make for a bittersweet elegy in this poignant and revealing drama. "… a work so perfectly judged it heralds the arrival of a major playwright … Greenberg is extraordinary." *–The NY Daily News* "Greenberg's play is filled with graceful passages that are by turns melancholy, harrowing, and often, quite funny." *–Variety* [2M, 1W] ISBN: 0-8222-1676-0

★ **THE WEIR by Conor McPherson.** In a bar in rural Ireland, the local men swap spooky stories in an attempt to impress a young woman from Dublin who recently moved into a nearby "haunted" house. However, the tables are soon turned when she spins a yarn of her own. "You shed all sense of time at this beautiful and devious new play." *–The NY Times* "Sheer theatrical magic. I have rarely been so convinced that I have just seen a modern classic. Tremendous." *–The London Daily Telegraph* [4M, 1W] ISBN: 0-8222-1706-6

**DRAMATISTS PLAY SERVICE, INC.**
440 Park Avenue South, New York, NY 10016  212-683-8960  Fax 212-213-1539
postmaster@dramatists.com   www.dramatists.com